Praise for

"There are circumstances in which prose is poetry, and the unornamented candor of Rosenblatt's writing slowly attains to a sober sort of lyricism. But this is more than just a moving book. It is also a useful book. Perhaps because beauty is the antithesis of use, there is something especially marvelous about useful beauty. *Making Toast*, a memoir of helpfulness, may actually help some of the people who read it. There are not many books that are important in this way: Helen Garner's *The Spare Room*, a shatteringly honest and artful account of assisting a friend through her dying, is another such book. The epigraph to Garner's austere masterpiece, from Elizabeth Jolley, captures also the large spirit of Rosenblatt's book: 'It is a privilege to prepare the place where someone else will sleep.' Rosenblatt's children and grandchildren chose their father and grandfather well. His toast is buttered with wisdom."          —Leon Wieseltier, *New Republic*

"Rosenblatt brings the reader to tears, but with prose that is as restrained as it is evocative.... Innocence and beauty restored then, with this gem of a memoir, deceptively simple in its proportions, but in truth: sad, funny, brave and luminous—see how it catches the light.... Without self-pity or sanctimony, the author reminds us in this rare and generous book that there is no remedy for death. The way to live, he concludes, is 'to value the passing time'; the best we can do is to pay attention and to love each other well."          —*Los Angeles Times*

"*Making Toast* is about coping with grief, caring for children and creating an ad hoc family for as long as this particular configuration is required, but mostly it's a textbook on what constitutes perfect writing and how to be a class act."          —Carolyn See, *Washington Post*

"Rosenblatt... sets a perfect tone and finds the right words to describe how his family is coping with their grief.... It may seem odd to call a book about such a tragic event charming, but it is. There is indeed life after death, and Rosenblatt proves that without a doubt."

—*USA Today*

"[An] exquisite, restrained little memoir filled with both hurt and humor." —NPR's *All Things Considered*

"Sad but somehow triumphant, this memoir is a celebration of family, and of how, even in the deepest sorrow, we can discover new links of love and the will to go on." —*O, The Oprah Magazine*

"Hauntingly lovely." —*Christian Science Monitor*

"This could have been a grim tale, but it is, instead, one of cautious optimism, deep love, and the kind of inner strength that gets us through the worst of times." —Pamela Fiori, *Town & Country*

"This memoir is a spare, simple account of a family coming to terms with its grief after a sudden death. But more than that, it's an extraordinarily evocative and unpretentious look at what it means to be a family, raise children, watch them grow and, sometimes, say good-bye to them." —*Jerusalem Post*

"Rosenblatt avoids the sentimentality that might have weighed down [*Making Toast*]; he writes with humor and an engagement with life that makes the occasional flashes of grief all the more telling. The result is a beautiful account of human loss, measured by the steady effort to fill in the void." —*Publishers Weekly* (starred review)

"Beautiful and moving." —*New York Times*

"Rosenblatt's clean, elegant prose is utterly devoid of sentimentality, which only makes his sharply drawn memories of his daughter and the anecdotes chronicled in the making of this newly constructed family all the more poignant." —*Observer*

"Rosenblatt, who has excelled in nearly every literary form—journalism, drama (six off-Broadway plays), nonfiction, and fiction—now adorns the memoir genre with a graceful, slim but piercing tale of loss and its sometimes grievous, sometimes ennobling effects.... Through the glass of the author's transparent style we see all the sharp and soft contours of grief."

—*Kirkus Reviews*

"A painfully beautiful memoir telling how grandparents are made over into parents, how people die out of order, how time goes backwards. Written with such restraint as to be both heartbreaking and instructive."

—E. L. Doctorow

"Written so forthrightly, but so delicately, that you feel you're a part of this family. Rosenblatt's writing turns a story that might be too uncomfortable to read, or too sentimental, in the direction of simple facts that require sophisticated, but instinctual, responses. How lucky some of us are to see clearly what needs to be done, even in the saddest, most life-altering circumstances."

—Ann Beattie

"Roger Rosenblatt means, I believe, to teach patience, love, a fondness for the quotidian, and a deftness for saving the lost moment—when faced with lacerating loss. These are brilliant lessons, fiercely learned. But Rosenblatt comes to them and to us—suitably—with immense humility."

—Richard Ford

"The blow of the improbable: a highly achieved daughter who is the mother of very young children is tragically struck down in her radiant prime. Husband, children, and grandparents are bereft, and what can come of such a maelstrom of grief? *Making Toast*, Roger Rosenblatt's piercing account of broken hearts, records how love, hurt, and responsibility can, through antic wit and tenderness, turn a shattered household into a luminous new-made family."

—Cynthia Ozick

# making
# toast

───◆───

a family story

───◆───

# roger rosenblatt

ecco

*An Imprint of HarperCollinsPublishers*

HarperCollins books may be purchased for educational, business, or sales promotional use. For information, please write: Special Markets Department, HarperCollins Publishers, 10 East 53rd Street, New York, NY 10022.

Portions of this work originally appeared in *The New Yorker.*

A hardcover edition of this book was published in 2010 by Ecco, an imprint of HarperCollins Publishers.

FIRST ECCO PAPERBACK EDITION PUBLISHED 2011.

*Designed by Suet Yee Chong*

The Library of Congress has cataloged the hardcover edition as follows:

Rosenblatt, Roger.
   Making toast : a family story / Roger Rosenblatt.—1st ed.
    p. cm.
   ISBN 978-0-06-182593-4
   1. Rosenblatt, Roger—Family. 2. Grandparents. 3. Grandparent and child. 4. Bereavement. 5. Parenting. 6. Grandparents as parents. 7. Daughters—Death. I. Title.

   [call number n/a]
   306.857 22

2010281167

ISBN 978-0-06-182595-8 (pbk.)

11   12   13   14   15   OV/RRD   10  9  8  7  6  5  4  3  2  1

for amy

The trick when foraging for a tooth lost in coffee grounds is not to be misled by the clumps. The only way to be sure is to rub each clump between your thumb and index finger, which makes a mess of your hands. For some twenty minutes this morning, Ginny and I have been hunting in the kitchen trash can for the top front left tooth of our seven-year-old granddaughter, Jessica. Loose for days but not yet dislodged, the tooth finally dropped into a bowl of Apple Jacks. I wrapped it for safekeeping in a paper napkin and put it on the kitchen counter, but it was mistaken for trash by Ligaya, Bubbies's nanny. Bubbies (James) is twenty months and the youngest of our daughter Amy's three children. Sammy, who is five, is uninterested in the tooth search, and Jessie is unaware of it. We hope to find the tooth so that Jessie won't worry about the Tooth Fairy not showing up.

This sort of activity has constituted our life since Amy died, on December 8, 2007, at 2:30 p.m., six months ago. Today is June 9, 2008. The day of her death, Ginny and I drove from our home in Quogue, on the south shore of Long Island, to Bethesda, Maryland, where Amy and her husband, Harris, lived. With Harris's encouragement, we have been there ever since. "How long are you staying?" Jessie asked the next morning. "Forever," I said.

———◆———

Amy Elizabeth Rosenblatt Solomon, thirty-eight years old, pediatrician, wife of hand surgeon Harrison Solomon, and mother of three, collapsed on her treadmill in the downstairs playroom at home. "Jessie and Sammy discovered her," our oldest son, Carl, told us on the phone. Carl lives in Fairfax, Virginia, not far from Amy and Harris, with his wife, Wendy, and their two boys, Andrew and Ryan. Jessie had run upstairs to Harris. "Mommy isn't talking," she said. Harris got to Amy within seconds, and tried CPR, but her heart had stopped and she could not be revived.

Amy's was ruled a "sudden death due to an anomalous right coronary artery"—meaning that her two coronary arteries fed her heart from the same side. Normally, the arteries are located on both sides of the heart so that if one fails, the other can do the work. In Amy's heart, they ran alongside each other. They could have been squeezed between the aorta and the pulmonary artery, which can expand during physical exercise. The blood flow was cut off. Her condition, affecting less than two thousandths of one percent of the population, was asymptomatic; she might have died at any time in her life.

She would have appreciated the clarity of the verdict. Amy was a very clear person, even as a small child, knowing intuitively what plain good sense a particular situation required. She had a broad expanse of forehead, dark, nearly black hair, and hazel eyes. Both self-confident and selfless, when she faced you there could be no doubt you were the only thing on her mind.

Her clarity could make her severe with her family, especially her two brothers. Carl and John, our youngest, withered when she excoriated them for such offenses as invading her room. She could also poke you gently with her wit. When she was about to graduate from the NYU School of Medicine, her class had asked me to be the speaker. A tradition of the school allows a past graduate to place the hood of the gown on a current graduate. Harris, who had graduated the previous year, was set to "hood" Amy. At dinner the night before the ceremony, a friend remarked, "Amy, isn't it great? Your dad is giving the graduation speech, and your fiancé is doing the hood." Amy said, "It is. And it's also pretty great that I'm graduating."

Yet her clarity also contributed to her kindness. When she was six, I was driving her and three friends to a birthday party. One of the girls got carsick. The other two backed away, understandably, with cries of "Ooh!" and "Yuck!" Amy drew closer to the stricken child, to comfort her.

———◆———

Ginny and I moved from a five-bedroom house, with a den and a large kitchen, to a bedroom with a connected bath—the in-law apartment in an alcove off the downstairs playroom that we used to occupy whenever we visited. We put in a dresser and a desk, and Harris added a

TV and a rug. It may have appeared that we were reducing our comforts, but the older one gets the less space one needs, and the less one wants. And we still have our house in Quogue.

I found I could not write and didn't want to. I could teach, however, and it helped me feel useful. I drive from Bethesda to Quogue on Sundays, and meet my English literature classes and MFA writing workshops at Stony Brook University early in the week, then back to Bethesda. The drive takes about five hours and a tank of gas each way. But it is easier and faster than flying or taking a train.

Road rage was a danger those early weeks. I picked fights with store clerks for no reason. I lost my temper with a student who phoned me too frequently about her work. I seethed at those who spoke of Amy's death in the clichés of modern usage, such as "passing" and "closure." I cursed God. In a way, believing in God made Amy's death more, not less, comprehensible, since the God I believe in is not beneficent. He doesn't care. A friend was visiting Jerusalem when he got the news about Amy. He kicked the Wailing Wall, and said, "Fuck you, God!" My sentiments exactly.

What's Jessie's favorite winter jacket? The blue

not the pink, though pink is her favorite color. Sammy prefers whole milk in his Froot Loops or MultiGrain Cheerios. He calls it "cow milk." Jessie drinks only Silk soy milk. She likes a glass of it at breakfast. Sammy prefers water. Such information had to be absorbed quickly. Sammy sees himself as the silver Power Ranger, Jessie is the pink. Sammy's friends are Nico, Carlos, and Kipper. Jessie's are Ally, Danielle, and Kristie. There were play-dates to arrange, birthday-party invitations to respond to, school forms to fill out. Sammy goes to a private preschool, the Geneva Day School; Jessie to Burning Tree, the local public school. We had to master their schedules.

I reaccustomed myself to things about small children I'd forgotten. Talking toys came back into my life. I will be walking with the family through an airport, and the voice of a ventriloquist's dummy in a horror movie will seep through the suitcase. Buzz Lightyear says, "To infinity and beyond!" A talking phone says, "Help me!" Another toy says, "I'm a pig. Can we stop?"

In all this, two things were of immeasurable use to us. First, Leslie Adelman, a friend of Amy's and Harris's, and the mother of friends of the children, created a Web site inviting others to prepare dinners for our family. Emails were sent by Leslie, our daughter-in-law Wendy, Laura Gwyn, another friend and school mother, and Betsy Mencher, who had gone to college with Amy. Soon one hundred people—school families, friends and colleagues of Amy's and Harris's, neighbors—comprised the list. Participants deposited dinners in a blue cooler outside our front door. Food was provided every other evening, with enough for the nights in between, from mid-December to the beginning of June.

The second was a piece of straightforward wisdom that Bubbies's nanny gave Harris. Ligaya is a small, lithe woman in her early fifties. I know little of her life except that she is from the Philippines, with a daughter there and a grown son here who is a supervisor in a restaurant, and that she has a work ethic of steel and the flexibility to deal with any contingency. She also shows a sense of practical formality by calling Bubbies James, and not by the nickname Amy had coined, to ensure the more respectable name for his future. Ligaya altered her schedule to be with us twelve hours a day, five days a week—an indispensable gift, especially to her small charge, who giggles with delight when he hears her key in the front door. No one outside the family could have felt Amy's death more acutely. Yet what she said to Harris, and to the rest of us, was dispassionate: "You are not the first to go through such a thing, and you are better able to handle it than most."

---

Bubbies looks around for Amy, says "Mama" when he sees her pictures, and clings to his father. Bubbies has blond hair and a face usually occupied by observant silences. When I am alone with him, he plays happily enough. I've taught him to give a high five, and when he does, I stagger across the room to show him how strong he is. He likes to take a pot from one kitchen cabinet and Zone bars from another, deposit the bars in the pot, and put back the lid. He'll do this contentedly for quite a while. When Harris enters the kitchen, Bubbies drops everything, runs to him, and holds him tight at the knees.

Jessie is tall, also blond, with an expression forever on the brink of enthusiasm. Amy used to say she was the most optimistic person she'd ever known. She is excited about her hip-hop dance class; about a concert her school is giving in Amy's name, to raise money for a memorial scholarship set up at the NYU School of Medicine; about going to the *Nutcracker.* "Do your Nutcracker dance, Boppo," Jessie says. (Ginny is Mimi, I am Boppo.) I swing into my improvised ballet, the high point of which is when I wiggle my ass like the dancing mice. Jessie is also excited about our trip to Disney World in January, the adventure that Amy and Harris had planned for themselves and the three children months before Amy died. We speak of distant summer plans in Quogue. Jessie is excited.

Sammy is tall, too, with dark hair and wide-set, ruminative eyes. He brings me a book to read, about a caterpillar. He brings another, which just happened to be in the house, called *Lifetimes: The Beautiful Way to Explain Death to Children.* The book says, "There's a beginning and an end for everything that is alive. In between is living." The book illustrates its lessons with pictures of birds, fish, plants, and people. I lean back on the couch with Sammy tucked in the crook of my arm, and read to him about the beauty of death.

———◆———

Like other nonreligious families, ours tends to cherry-pick among the holidays, adopting those features that most appeal to children—eggs and the Bunny at Easter, the tree and Santa at Christmas. Characteristically, Amy had prepared for Christmas long in advance. Unwrapped gifts for Jessie, Sammy, and Bubbies lay hidden in the house. Traditional ornaments and ones she made herself had been taken out of their annual storage. There were little painted claylike figures representing a family standing in a row and singing carols, and pictures of her own family as it had grown every year, along with older ornaments that Ginny and I had given her. Amy and Harris had picked out their tree the morning of the day she died. It remained on the deck during our first days of mourning, leaning against a post at a forty-degree angle, the trunk soaking in a bucket of water. Eventually we brought it indoors, and concentrated on making the holiday appear as normal as possible.

On Christmas Eve, Ginny cooked a turkey for Harris, me, and John, who was down from New York for a few days. I read Jessie and Sammy *The Night Before Christmas* as I had done with our own three children, adding nonsense exigeses and pretending to take issue with words such as "coursers" in an effort to hold their attention. Last year they had become restive by the time I got to ". . . and all through the house." This year they listened to the whole thing. When the children were asleep, Ginny, Harris, and I opened some of the toys that Santa was about to bring. Jessie still believes, because she wants to. She got an American Girl doll; Sammy, Power Ranger outfits and DVDs; Bubbies, a remote control dog like a beagle puppy, that walked, sat, and yipped. Harris set up the some-assembly-required toys. It took him half an hour to put together an electric race track that would have taken me half a day when I was a young father. And *his* structure did not collapse. He and the children had decorated the tree as well. He strung the white lights.

Carl and Wendy and their boys usually spend Christmas with Wendy's family in Pittsburgh, so they came over the day before Christmas Eve to exchange presents. Carl and I gave Harris tickets to the Masters golf tournament coming up in April. He had always wanted to go. We got him two tickets so that he could take a friend. As we later learned, he had planned to go with Amy the following year to celebrate his fortieth birthday. Because it was a last-minute thought, we were not able to get the actual tickets, which we'd reserved, so Carl made up an elegant presentation of the gift, worded like the announcement of a prize. The lettering stood out against a background of the Masters course in Augusta. We wanted to hide the gift in a bright green sports jacket like the ones Masters winners are awarded, but we couldn't find one. We had to settle for an olive-green windbreaker. When we presented it to Harris, he thought the windbreaker was his gift and was happy with it. We told him to look in the inside pocket. He held the piece of paper in his hands, stood, and burst into tears.

---

Getting the Masters tickets was Carl's idea. He does things like that. In a way, he is a fusion of Amy's characteristics, and of Harris's as well—always looking out for others, yet smoothly capable in all that he does. He has the honest, supple face of the guy who makes you feel welcome in strange places, who calls out your name in the crowd and beckons. After college he started out as a sports writer, but hit a dead end. He fell into business and immediately rose to high executive positions, without the benefit of an MBA. He makes those under him feel useful and appreciated. He is a gentleman. He thrives as a father. And he is the fastest learner I have ever seen. As a three-year-old, he picked up fractions by studying the odometer in our car as it advanced one tenth of a mile at a time. When making his computations, he looked entranced, as he does today if I ask him to figure out what is to me a math problem. He seems to recollect every minute of his childhood. Most of his memories are good, fortunately for Ginny and me, who tend mainly to recall our mistakes. His recollections of Amy—a moment of petulance or of exasperation at him—are very funny. His hair is graying.

————◆————

It is January, 2008. In the late afternoon in our hotel room in Disney World, Ginny sits on the bed with Bubbies in her arms. He is asleep at last, after a couple of hours of running on a lawn and away from us every time we tried to get him back in the stroller. When I was alone with him yesterday, he took a header on a pathway, cried lustily for a couple of minutes, then insisted I put him down so that he could continue running in the wintry air. This is the coldest it has been in central Florida in many years.

While Harris took Jessie and Sammy to Space Mountain, we stayed with Bubs, who launched into another round of perpetual motion. Amy used to say, "James, you're out of control." Eventually he tired, and I carried him up to our room, where he got a second wind and ran around some more. I fed him pieces of apple, which were hard, so I chewed them a little first. Finally, he fell asleep.

Jessie had been so worked up about this trip, she had told her classmates the dates they were planning to go. Amy happened to be volunteering in her class that day. The school principal was also visiting the class. When Jessie blurted out the dates of the forthcoming trip, the principal looked aghast. "Oh, you can't go on *those* days, Jessie," she said. "They're *school* days." Amy, trying to hide behind one of the children's desks, gave a meek and friendly wave.

The light from the window is pale and cold. The TV is off. No sounds emit from the hotel corridor. All is still in Disney World. Ginny sits at the end of the bed with her back to me. I see the back of her head and the top of Bubbies's just above her left shoulder.

We begin to fit in to Amy's and Harris's house. We knew the house only as visiting family, having stayed for a few days at a time, perhaps a week. Now it is ours without belonging to us, familiar and strange. We learn how to lock the glass door between the kitchen and the deck. We learn how to operate the dishwasher, the thermostat. We learn where the tools, the extension cords, the Scotch tape, and the light bulbs are kept. We note the different dresser drawers for the children's clothing, the location of favored books and games, such as Balloon Lagoon, Cariboo, The Uncle Wiggily Game, and Perfection. Since one of Bubbies's many occupations is to reach into the games cabinet and spill the contents on the floor, often losing the crucial pieces, learning where the games are stored soon becomes beside the point.

Ginny handles most of the essentials. She lays out the children's outfits for the day, supervises the brushing of teeth, braids Jessie's hair, and checks the backpacks. There is hardly a moment when she is not on call. Harris gave her Amy's cell phone, for which Ginny recorded her own greeting. Whoever gets the answering machine hears, "Hi. You have reached 301 . . ." and then, "Mimi!"—Jessie needing something in the middle of Ginny's recording.

I do odd jobs, such as driving the kids to appointments, and food shopping at Whole Foods or Giant. Occasionally I contribute an idea. Shortly after Amy died, I instituted the "Word for the Morning." At the start of the day, I write a word on a yellow Post-it, which I stick to the side of a wooden napkin holder on the kitchen table. Usually I make a game of the word, asking Jessie and Sammy to find other words in it, or I include a drawing. When the morning's word was "equestrian," I drew a horse that looked a lot like a horse. I try to hit upon a word that is a stretch for Sammy but not too easy for Jessie, and when I can think of one, a word with an interesting element, such as a silent letter. The first Word for the Morning was "answer." Sammy said, "Tomorrow, give us a silly word, Boppo." The word for the following morning was "poopies."

———◆———

I wake up earlier than the others, usually around 5 a.m., to perform the one household duty I have mastered. After posting the morning's word, emptying the dishwasher, setting the table for the children's breakfasts, and pouring the MultiGrain Cheerios or Froot Loops or Apple Jacks or Special K or Fruity Pebbles, I prepare toast. I take out the butter to allow it to soften, and put three slices of Pepperidge Farm Hearty White in the toaster oven. Bubbies and I like plain buttered toast; Sammy prefers it with cinnamon, with the crusts cut off. When the bell rings, I shift the slices from the toaster to plates, and butter them.

Harris usually spends half the night in Bubbies's little bed. When I go upstairs, around 6 a.m., Bubbies hesitates, but I give him a knowing look and he opens his arms to me. "Toast?" he says. I take him from his father, change him, and carry him downstairs to allow Harris another twenty minutes' sleep.

———◆———

Sammy remains matter-of-fact. One late afternoon, we watch television together. A mother appears on the show. "No mom for me," he says. In the beginning, we tried explaining that Amy continued to live in our thoughts and memories. "Mommy is still with us," I said. Sammy asked where, exactly. He indicated a point in the air. "Is Mommy there?" I said yes. He indicated another point. "There?" I said yes. I said, "She's always with us, every-where. We can't see her, but we can feel her spirit." He said, "There?"

———◆———

While Ligaya and Ginny look after Bubbies and Sammy, I take Jessie to the bus stop. On a damp gray morning we stand together at the corner of our street. One by one, down the hill come the mothers of the neighborhood, their kids running beside them. An impromptu soccer game develops. Jessie joins in. The scene passes for pleasant and ordinary, unless one notes the odd presence of the lone grandfather.

With luck, Ginny and I will live to see all three children grow into adults, and Jessie will become a teenager and throw fits about boyfriends and stamp her feet and yell that we don't understand a thing, not a thing. But today I help her with her oversize pink backpack, and her little umbrella with pink butterflies before she boards the school bus. And I stand looking as the bus drives off, and tell the mothers to have a good day.

———◆———

The house Amy and Harris bought in 2004 was a sand-yellow Colonial, built in the 1960s, and it had substance—

a family home for a lifetime. The walls were thick, the hardwood floors level, the oak, black walnut, and poplar trees in the backyard, old. Though reared in cities, Amy had always wanted a house in the suburbs. Harris grew up in Bethesda, and went to Burning Tree and to Walt Whitman High School, which is less than a quarter of a mile from the house. His affection for his hometown suited Amy well. Whenever Ginny and I drove down, we phoned her from the car when we were a few minutes away. She would stand framed by the dark-red doorway, holding a child or two. Everyone smiled.

She practiced medicine only two days a week, to be with the children. Her household was like her—full of play, but careful. In the storage area downstairs, there was always a surplus of bandages, paper napkins, cups, coffee filters, paper towels, and Kleenex, as well as batteries of every size. To this day, we have not run out of Advil.

She had a gift for custom and ceremony—the qualities Yeats wished for in "A Prayer for My Daughter." She chronicled the children's first years by taking pictures of them in each of their first twelve months, and framing them for the walls of their rooms. The details of birthdays and holidays were important to her—a Dora the Explorer party for Jessie, for which Amy made a treasure map; a Bob the Builder party for Sammy, for which she got hard hats. On the Thanksgiving before she died, seventeen family members arrived, including Harris's parents, Dee and Howard, and his older sister Beth, and Wendy's parents, Rose and Bob Huber. There were many cooks, not too many, all toiling under Amy's supervision. Harris, Howard, Bob, Carl, John, and I watched as much football as we were permitted. The hand surgeon carved the turkey, his skill with a knife impressive and creepy. We took our seats at the table. We clasped our glasses. During the previous year, Howard had had a heart valve repaired, and I was treated successfully for prostate cancer and melanoma. Harris raised a toast to the family's renewed health.

———◆———

Harris's stoicism is undemonstrative. A strong man, built wide and powerful, he easily carries all three children at once in his arms up the stairs. The sight of his back makes me sad. He performs surgery two days a week and heads orthopedics at Holy Cross Hospital. At home, his few remaining hours are devoted to working out the children's schedules with Ginny and Ligaya, and playing games and watching Sponge Bob with the kids. He bathes them and tucks them in.

On the day Amy died, he had sat beside her body in the hospital—an hour, maybe more. Now, he rarely speaks about his feelings. He and I talk about sports and politics, agreeing over half the time on both. We talk a lot about the children. Ginny tells me that when I am away, and she and Harris sit down to their late dinner in the kitchen, her heart breaks for him. "This should be his wife sitting across the table," she says.

He says he doubts that he'll remarry. Self-sufficient, he tends to be a world within himself. He fixes things like lamps and toilets. He sews. He solves problems with electrical wires and fuses. He makes the hands of others work again. And he has done everything one can do in his situation—encouraging the children to talk about Amy whenever they feel like it, and not to hold back tears. Whenever necessary, he and the children visit a psychotherapist who specializes in grief counseling. He keeps in close contact with Jessie's and Sammy's teachers. But he also deserves a life.

He embraces the demands put upon him with a gusto that dispenses cheer, and in the lulls we try to keep one another afloat. One night in February, Jessie and Sammy had a meltdown as they were going to bed. Ginny and I sat in the living room, listening to Harris's steady voice in the intermissions of the children's wailing. Eventually, they were quieted. He came downstairs and sat staring vacantly at his laptop. "Look," I said, going over to him. "We're never going to get over this. That's a given. But the children will be all right. I promise you. I've seen it elsewhere."

"I'm a scientist," he said. "It's hard for me to deal with things that aren't facts."

———◆———

Amy used to say, "Harris makes do," twisting his ability to adjust to uncomfortable or difficult circumstances into a failing. He retaliated by ribbing her about her perfectionism. Once, when Carl asked him how Amy liked their new cable TV and Internet system, Harris said, "Amy hates everything." He told me she had set the North American record for excessively particular coffee orders at Starbucks. The orders varied according to the seasons. Her winter order was triple grande, skim gingerbread latte. Her summer order was iced venti Americano with room, and four pumps of sugar-free vanilla.

It figured. When Amy was no more than three years old, and we would stop at McDonald's on a trip, she would order her hamburger plain. Since orders for a plain hamburger were not anticipated in the billion hamburgers prepared by McDonald's daily all over America, it took as long as twenty-five minutes for the fast food restaurant to dish one up.

"You know, Amy, when I was a little girl . . ."

"Oh, Daddy!"—tired of the joke.

On one occasion, we were driving to New York from Cambridge, where I was teaching at Harvard. It was the day before Thanksgiving so the trip took hours longer than usual. After our interminable wait for Amy's hamburger, she decided she would also like a piece of McDonald's apple pie. She was taking her sweet time with that, too. I told her, "Hurry up, A." (We called her A.) She tossed her pie in the trash. When we arrived at my parents' apartment, my younger brother Peter asked Amy how she'd enjoyed the trip. She said, "Daddy didn't let me finish my pie."

Amy and Harris could kid each other without risk because their marriage was like a solid tennis doubles team. Neither one had to look to see where the other was standing on the court. A few years ago, on a Saturday night, Ginny and I baby-sat while they went to a medical benefit dinner. They almost never had the time or energy to go out, or dress up, though, like most young parents, they seemed indefatigable. Before leaving, they stood together in the hallway. They looked stunning. Another time, we drove down from Quogue to take care of the three children. Bubbies was eleven months old. Amy and Harris went off to Bermuda with Liz and James Hale, longtime friends from medical school. When they returned after four days, Ginny and I were flopped on the sectional, barely sentient. We greeted them with a popular song of that year, altering the lyrics: "They tried to make us go to rehab. We said yes, yes, yes!"

———

Ginny taught kindergarten and first grade in Cambridge and in Washington, D.C., during the early years of our marriage. Now she volunteers in the children's schools, as Amy did. She helps Jessie with her homework. I watch them at the kitchen table, bent over a book, and overhear their soft talking. Ginny asks, "How does the chrysalis protect itself against predators?" Jessie says, "It shakes to scare them off."

I do puzzle books with Jessie, and Sammy peppers me with questions about animals and the stars and planets. I can't answer most of his questions. "What are afternoons like on Jupiter?" he asks me. I have to look that up.

I am often confounded by something else I'd forgotten about children: they have no respect for sequential thought. Responding to one of their relentless questions, I will go as deep as I can into an explanation of, say, a solar eclipse. Sammy will ask, "What's the biggest number in the world?" At the same time, Jessie will ask, "How tall will I be, Boppo?" Then, Sammy: "Do marlins have lips?"

"So when the moon moves between the earth and the sun . . ."

"What are you talking about, Boppo?"

Bubbies has been attending to his own education, proceeding from one word, to several, to two-word sentences, to three and more. Some say that children learn to speak in order to tell the stories already in them. An early word of his was "back." He wanted reassurance that when any of us left the house, or even a room, we were coming back. He has always used one-word sentences to his advantage, his vocabulary consisting mainly of references to things he favors—the mower, the stove, birds, bananas. The single words suit his despotic streak. "Outside" means "Let's move it, Boppo!"

———◆———

Jessie's first-grade teacher, Coleen Carone, has me visit the class at the Burning Tree School to talk about writing. Ms. Carone is young and hip, with dancing and darting eyes. She calls the kids "Baby." Jessie introduces me to her classmates, who sit with their hands folded on their desks and give me the once-over. "This is my grandfather. We call him Boppo." The children discuss stories they are working on. I begin to suspect I am out of my depth.

Ms. Carone asks me, "How is character developed, Boppo?" I bumble through an answer involving matters of consistency and variation in character development. The more I temper my language, the more befuddled I sound. My discourse is greeted with polite stares. Jessie is proud of me anyway, and stands at my side. Ms. Carone looks at me brightly, as if to say, "Don't worry. We'll take it from here." She asks the children to consider a main character, then list his or her qualities—loyal, jealous, rude, brave, generous. Each child stands before the class to answer questions. Arthur writes about a superhero.

"Anything you'd like to ask Arthur?" Ms. Carone says to the others.

One girl asks, "Does your superhero tell the truth?"

Arthur thinks and says yes.

"Always?" the girl asks.

———◆———

Late in February, I have a literary "conversation" with Alice McDermott as part of a series at the 92nd Street Y in New York, in which I ask writers questions about their work. Alice and I sit in chairs angled toward each other on a large stage in an auditorium. Hundreds of people look up at us. Usually, I feel comfortable at such events, more so than in less heightened social situations, because when you're at the center of a public event, you're alone. This being my first time in public after Amy's death, however, I feel tense and out of place. Alice's gentleness and thoughtfulness put me at ease.

We talk about *After This*, her novel about the Keane family, whose son is killed in Vietnam. The novel centers not on the death, but rather on the family's grief, which challenges their faith in God. I ask Alice what God has to do with it. Isn't life just luck, good and bad? She says we have to believe in God's overarching good will. "Even as we face unbearable sorrow," she says, "small things happen that make us able to bear it. John and Mary Keane face the greatest tragedy that a couple could face, and yet things happen in their lives that bring them back to moments of joy." Alice ascribes such moments to God's benevolence. I cannot tell if she sees that I do not.

————◆————

Whenever the inspiration strikes, I launch into the "Boppo National Anthem," which had its debut in Bethesda a couple of years ago and appeared an immediate success due to the composer's exuberance:

> *Boppo the Great!*
> *Boppo the Great!*
> *I can't wait for Boppo the Great!*
> *I hope he's not late!*

Sometimes, Sammy will change the last line to "I hope he's not stinky," indicating that adoption of the anthem will not be universal. When I tell him I plan

to teach the anthem to his entire school, he looks terrified. "In real life? But there are five hundred kids in the
school!"

"Yes! Think of it!" I tell him. "Five hundred children,
all singing 'Boppo the Great'! You'll be so proud. And
you *do* love that song!"

"I *hate* it!" he says. "I only sing it to make you happy."
I grab him and sing "The Laughing Drum," another
original ditty, to which I play his tummy like a tom-tom,
and tickle him silly.

Amy would make up songs for the children, too. She
used to sing, or chant:

> *Sammer, Sammer, you're the one*
> *Sammer, Sammer, you're so fun.*
> *Sammer, Sammer, you're so sweet.*
> *You've got big toes and little feet.*

Carl used to inform her that "you're so fun" was a
poor use of English and suggested that the addition of
"much" before "fun" would constitute a grammatical and
literary improvement. Amy would let him know how
she appreciated his constructive criticism. I thought her
song cute, though, as I told her, I felt it lacked the gran-
deur of an anthem.

———◆———

Just before Jessie was born, Amy asked Ginny and me and Dee and Howard, what our grandparental names would be. Everyone else chose something sensible. Ginny chose "Mimi," after her own grandmother. I chose "El Guapo"—the handsome one—the nickname of an ineffective former Red Sox relief pitcher. As a Yankee fan, I appreciated El Guapo's ineffectiveness. Amy disapproved of the name, but let it slide. Things worked out in her favor. The babies could not pronounce El Guapo, thus Boppo. "Such a sad story," said Amy. "He thought of himself as the handsome one, but he became a clown."

Yet the name has advantages. One morning Jessie had Hannah Montana's "Nobody's Perfect" cranked up to an obliterating level. "Turn it down, Jess," I told her. She obliged by grudgingly diminishing the volume one-hundredth of a millimeter. I scowled. She lowered the noise even less. "Turn it down, Jess!" She stomped over to the CD player, turned it off with a dramatic flick of the hand, stormed upstairs, and would not speak to me for much of the rest of the day. She was also grumpy with a playmate. "What's the matter with you?" I overheard

Harris ask her. She said, "I'm mad at Boppo!" How long can one be mad at Boppo?

---

"Won't anyone in this family play Twister with me?" Jessie stands before the sectional in the TV room on which Ginny, Harris, and I sit. Ginny and Harris remain mute. "Won't anyone in this family ever play Twister with me?"—her voice plaintive, her palms turned upward like an evangelical preacher's. Not a word or gesture from Ginny or Harris. "I'll play with you, Jess," I say—forgetting why Twister is called Twister. Harris chuckles malevolently. "Oh thank you, Boppo!" says Jess. "You're the only one in this whole entire family who ever plays with me!"

---

Carl picks me up at the house, and we drive to the Verizon Center in downtown Washington, to watch a Georgetown basketball game. One of the bright spots of our new living arrangement is that Ginny and I get to see more of him, Wendy, and the boys. He tells me that

Amy had called Wendy on the Wednesday before she died, and that she had left a long message on their answering machine. "I kept A's message," he says. "Would you like to hear it?" I tell him no. "I understand," he says. "But if you change your mind, let me know. The message is so Amy. She was buying Christmas presents for Andrew and Ryan, but as she was talking, she remembered that they might overhear her message. So she was trying to tell Wendy what the presents were without coming out with it. It's very funny. Nothing sad. It actually makes me happy to listen to it." I tell him thanks, but no.

———

Carl, John, and I had stood together on the deck in Bethesda the day after Amy died, and wept. Arms around one another, we formed a circle, like skydivers, our garments flapping in the wind. I could not recall seeing either of them cry since they were very young. I am not sure they had ever seen me cry, except on sentimental occasions. John's tears came to rest on his cheeks. He looks a lot like Carl, but his features are sharper. He is dryly funny, like his sister, but his wit is proactive. He has an ear for cultural bullshit, and mimics clichés in a sonorous, mock-serious voice. Ginny and I rely on him for assessments of current movies. Like Carl, he is gracious with others. Like Carl, too, he is zealous about sports and will threaten to annihilate the TV screen whenever there's a bad call or a bonehead play. The two brothers are very close, as they were with Amy. She was nearly three years younger than Carl and nine years older than John, and her force of character seemed to civilize the two of them. The trouble with a close family is that it suffers closely, too. I stood with my two sons in the cold and put my arms around them, feeling the shoulders of men.

———◆———

Carl's boys have been made apprehensive by Amy's death. Seeing that it is possible to lose a mother, they fret when Wendy is out of the house, asking frequently where she is and when she is returning. They watch at the window. They brood about Amy. Three-year-old Ryan told Carl, "I wish I could jump to the sky." Ryan is big, born at just under ten pounds and growing at a giant's rate ever since. He sometimes thinks of himself as a superhero with superheroic powers. "Why do you want to jump to the sky?" Carl asked him. "I'd jump up and grab Aunt Amy and bring her back," he said.

—◆—

Neither Wendy nor Amy had sisters, but they found one in each other. It was fun to hear the two of them laugh and conspire. If you were walking behind them, they looked like twins—same height, same build, with their heads tilted toward each other. Wendy favors family over work, as Amy did, and gave up a position as a senior health policy analyst when she had children. She is direct, like Amy, one of those people who answers the question you ask. She also keeps me in line the way Amy did. One summer, she brought me a gift of Trivial Pursuit—the "Know-It-All" edition. Yet the two women were just different enough to make their friendship interesting. In her eulogy, Wendy told a story of Amy's amused, sardonic reaction to the environmentally pure paper Wendy used in her home. Risa Huber, her sister-in-law, was with them. Risa picked up a sheet of the paper, which disintegrated at the touch. "What's this?" she asked. "Exactly," said Amy. When Amy died, Wendy told Carl, "We're all angry. But no one is angrier than A."

There are things I don't want to know and things Ginny doesn't want to know. The doctors we consulted after Amy's death differed just enough in their speculations to leave room for anguish. Ginny wants to pursue the question to get to a more definite answer. I have hesitated. I do not wish to hear how extraordinarily rare Amy's condition was, and how even rarer it is that someone dies from it. One cardiologist I spoke with early on said flat out that however unlikely it is that someone was born with Amy's heart structure, the anomaly is almost never lethal. To find out, definitively, that Amy's death was one in a million or a trillion would only deepen my anger.

On the other hand, Ginny declined to view the open casket before the funeral. The funeral director had asked if we'd wanted the casket opened, and, having no practice in such choices, Harris and I said we did—for the pre-service "viewing," but not for the service itself. Harris, Carl, Wendy, John, and I, and Amy's and Harris's friends, the Hales, attended the viewing. Ginny would not. She did not want that to be her last image of Amy.

She may have been right. The figure in the casket—her hair done like Amy's, wearing Amy's new favorite brown dress and a shawl with tones of brown and red—seemed less our daughter than a semblance. One by one we approached to say our goodbyes. Out of habit, I touched her hair.

◆

Harris buys Sammy a punching bag, an Everlast heavy bag, which hangs on chains from the ceiling in the playroom. When Sammy isn't using it, I do.

◆

Ginny and I met in junior high school, and have known each other for more than fifty years. Laughing noisily with my friends, I looked up from my desk and saw the new girl, the first elegant thirteen-year-old since the British monarchs. Yet she has remained something of a mystery to me. She is without vanity. When I ask her about this, she says simply, "I was lucky to be born with a beautiful face." What might sound outrageous or wishful thinking in someone else seems a factual self-assessment.

She does have a beautiful face, the kind movie directors of the 1930s and 1940s might have looked for. It is not the siren's beautiful face, or the ingénue's; it is the face of intelligent virtue into which you read qualities such as competence, endurance, and acceptance of one's lot, along with a veiled sexiness—the face of the good wife and mother. Claudette Colbert had such a face, as did Joan Fontaine and Irene Dunne. Ginny is more beautiful than all of them. She acknowledges her looks as a way of dismissing their importance. Vanity is inapplicable to her life.

She has never had a lift or a tuck or a Botox treatment. "My hair and my nails," she says. "I'm vain about them"—meaning she has them done when she has the time. The subject of self-indulgence comes up with us these days because it is out of the question. Before Amy died, the big decision of our day was where to have lunch. "Our friends live by choice," she says. "What choice do I have?" The question is asked with a kind of satisfaction, in spite of the horror that occasioned it.

"I think my whole life has led up to this moment," she tells me. "When Carl was born, I felt I was coming into my own, to be a mother. It's what I love to do. I know who I am." Her motherly decisions are without premeditation, like an athlete's. When Bubbies starts school, she will take him every day, and not relegate that duty to Ligaya, because she knows that as able as Ligaya is, Mimi will be as close to a mother as Bubbies, Jessie, and Sammy will have from now on. "I'm comfortable doing this," she says. "And neither of us would have been able to pull it off if we hadn't been around a lot before Amy died."

There are outlets for her. She writes poems from time to time, and takes photographs. She founded a book club with Meredith Brokaw, consisting of some twenty remarkable women who have kept in constant touch since Amy's death. At a surprise birthday party for Ginny, their toasts were funny and touching, yet all of a piece—tributes to her selflessness. She maintains such friends because, like Amy, she listens to them. If someone tells her something, good or bad, she never tries to top it with a story of her own in those pointless competitions many people enter into, but rather concentrates on the person who seeks her attention. I had always thought of selflessness as a characteristic one learns and adopts, but in Ginny it seems like part of her genetic information. And now, in sorrow, she is in her element. "I am leading Amy's life," she says in despair yet comfort, too.

After forty-six years of marriage, due to the most painful of reasons, I am getting to know my wife.

———◆———

Back in Quogue, I meet with Kevin Stakey, the contractor Ginny and I hired to turn the garage into a playhouse for the grandchildren. We wanted a place where they could paint, work with clay, race cars, transform Transformers, and fight over card games like Uno and War. The plans were made in the late summer, with Amy, Harris, Carl, Wendy, and John involved. After Amy died, creating the playhouse became therapy for me. I hoped she would approve. It was my way of bringing her back to life. Because I could not understand why she died, I sought to make other things less confusing. I cleaned out junk-closets, gave order to a chaotic shelf of CDs, and cleared an ivy-choked area of the yard.

Kevin is in his late forties and built like a substantial piece of rope, the kind that ties ships to piers. He has a large head and a mustache and a beard on his chin, thick as a shoe brush. Shorter than I, at about five-foot, nine inches, he is twice as wide. When we shake hands, mine disappears in his. He took the news about Amy as if he had known her. I tell him that, because of our changed circumstances, I will not be around that much. He will have to make many decisions about the playhouse on his own.

"No problem," he says.

"Of course, if you screw up, I'll make you do it over."

"No problem."

"And don't fool around with the Yankees grill cover," I tell him. It was a Christmas gift from Harris. A Mets fan, Kevin has threatened to loosen the ties so that the wind would carry it away.

The building of the playhouse proceeded with little help needed from me. Kevin converted the garage by exposing the old beams of the original stable, putting up sheetrock, remaking the old windows, and replacing the dirty, cracked cement floor with gleaming wood. When he finished, I told him the brown of the wood had too much orange in it. "Can you fix it?"

"No problem," he said.

"Tell me, Kevin. If I asked you to turn the playhouse upside down, so the kids could enter from the roof, would that be a problem?"

"No problem," he said. He sanded the prestained

floor down to the wood, and made it the darker color I wanted.

———◆———

Harris's introduction to the family occurred in Quogue shortly before he and Amy became engaged. Amy had had a parade of boyfriends in high school and college, one of whom was "serious"—a genial, laid-back athlete who fitted in with us comfortably. We liked him and his family, and could picture Amy married to him in a seamless extension of their easygoing companionship. But whatever little thought I gave to their future suggested that theirs would not have been a marriage of people who improved each other or teased each other gainfully or made each other alert to the world's surprises, pleasant, foolish, and tragic. I never went so far as to picture them having children.

But when Harris entered Amy's life, and ours, here was a husband, a father, and a man full grown. For Carl, John, and me, he was instantly recognizable as one of the guys, but there was something else he had, like a secret soul. Exceptional people are sometimes freakish.

Harris seemed to have planed the edges of his exceptional qualities so as to prevent them from being offensive to others or isolating to himself. I see something similar in Sammy, as he tries to find a middle ground between his private silences and his fun. Harris walked into our house bringing not a perfectly fitting piece of the puzzle, but rather an eccentric enlargement of the whole. Wendy had had the same effect on us a year or so earlier.

Not that any of that stood in the way of the men of the house from turning Harris's introduction into a hazing. We swept him into our sloppy-yet-brutal game of two-on-two basketball, in which he held his own in terms of both sloppiness and brutality. Then came the essay question. Carl was a rabid fan of Patrick Ewing, the New York Knicks center. He named his yellow lab Ewing. I liked the dog but judged the human Ewing—who only passed the ball to his teammates out of desperation or forgetfulness—to be the main reason the Knicks never won a championship during his tenure. Without stating our antipodal positions on the matter, we asked Harris what he thought of Patrick Ewing. He looked from one of us to the other and said, "Terrible" to me. To Carl he said, "Superstar."

———◆———

One evening in the summer of 2007, Harris arrived at the Quogue house with Sammy and Jessie. Amy was slower coming in from the car with Bubs. The two older kids rushed in and Ginny and I greeted them on our knees with hugs and hollers. Belatedly, I realized that Harris was standing there too. I looked up. He said, "None taken."

———◆———

Harris maintains control of his emotions, his household, his job, and his children, because he must. But occasionally the effort shows. One day a drinking glass shattered on the kitchen floor. I started to pick up the bigger pieces to make it easier to vacuum the smaller ones. He shouted at me to get out of the kitchen so that he could vacuum the floor by himself. He never shouts. It may be that the hand surgeon was concerned that I would cut myself, but, in that small crisis, it felt more that he was asserting his authority—not because of a lack of self-confidence, but rather as a way of holding his life together.

Yet the presence of another man in his house who, like him, is accustomed to doing things his own way, cannot help but challenge his authority, even if I never actively challenge it. I do not wish to constitute one more source of pressure on him. And even if I felt the urge to put in my two cents, there would be little need, since he is capable of dealing with most mishaps. Only during the first week after Amy died did he rely on me to take the lead in managing the funeral and the burial. After that, one could almost see him physically steel himself and haul himself into shape. Always heavy though not fat, he must have lost twenty pounds in the past couple of months. He has cut down on coffee in the morning. To my regret, he has stopped eating toast.

As with us all, sorrow frames his every activity, and Harris's way of showing his feelings is to grow very quiet, as if closing a hatch. I tell him that if he ever wants to talk I am happy to do it. He appreciates the opening, but answers, "What is there to say?" Which is true, yet not entirely true. Catherine Andrews, the children's psychotherapist, also sees adults in grief. My guess is that Harris will consult her sooner or later, probably later.

I, too, may consult Catherine, since anger and emptiness remain my principal states of mind, especially when I am away from Ginny and the children, and alone in our house in Quogue. What keeps me from seeking Catherine's help is that unlike other psychological problems, what happened to Amy, and to all of us, is real. The monster is real. And while there may be strategies that help Ginny and me feel a little better rather than a little worse, we will never feel right again. No analysis or therapy will change that. I think Harris knows this, too. He is used to being on his own, but he never could have anticipated the depths of his current loneliness. It hurts and confounds him. He may appear enigmatic because he now sees that the course of his life—not unlike Ginny's—has prepared him to live without a main source of happiness, making him an enigma to himself.

———◆———

In a rare tranquil moment on a March afternoon, I sit on the green couch in the lower-level play area, rereading Anne Tyler's *The Accidental Tourist*. It is around four-thirty, and the light has gone from the day. Jessie comes downstairs and asks why I am so quiet. "I'm reading," I tell her. She takes one of her own books from the coffee table and sits beside me, extending her long legs over the front of the couch. We sit in silence, reading, five feet from where Amy collapsed and died. I look up from time to time, then return to my book.

Sammy hurtles downstairs and demands to know where his knight outfit is. Amazingly, I spot the outfit, which consists of silver pants, a shirt of mail, a shield, a sword, and a helmet with a visor. Sammy puts it on at once, lowers the visor over his face, and parades back and forth before the couch.

Jessie drops her book and plays a song from *High School Musical 2* at full blast on the stereo. She dances in front of the couch as Sir Sammy marches. Bubbies climbs down the stairs, Ligaya trailing behind him. He dances, too.

———◆———

Bubbies warms to me. Among the adults of the household I stand a distant fourth in his affections to Harris, Ginny, and Ligaya, and he continues to regard me accurately, as an amateur entertainer. Yet little by little he has detected that I have certain practical uses, in addition to toast-making, and as long as I keep my place, and perform the few duties of which I am capable, everything is okay.

I love his voice. He speaks the way I imagine Paul Newman sounded as a baby—with a slight husky rasp—and every statement is authoritative. His *questions* are authoritative. He also has a good ear, and pronounces all the syllables of longer words, such as "chocolate." Often he sounds like a southern European learning English: "cho-co-laht," emphasizing all syllables equally. He calls his sister "Jess-see-kah." I will say, "Jessica is sharing her water with you. What do you say, Bubs?" He says, "Thank you, Jess-see-kah."

Ginny frowns upon my roughhousing with him, but I did it with Carl, Amy, and John. We perform the "upside-down baby boy," which is what it sounds like. I hold him upside down over the bed, and swing him around by his ankles. I also perform the "flying baby boy," when I lie on my back on the bed with my legs raised and balance him on the bottoms of my feet. And I give him the "squeak," my word for a quick tickle. These assaults are welcomed gladly, except when he is intent on some matter of business—climbing up on the couch in order to jump off, or "cleaning" the floors with a length of hose from the vacuum cleaner. If, during any of those missions, I grab him to give him a squeak, he will protest—"No, Boppo!"—as if to remind me that he is not a toy. If I behave myself, and if there is no one better around, he will climb onto my lap, and take my face in his hands.

Here's a book for Bubs. Margaret Wise Brown's *Little Fur Family*. Garth Williams's drawings are fuzzy, in dusty, muted colors. Their spareness gives them life: the tree home of the fur family, and its curtained windows and green shutters and red door with its own little green roof; the nearby stream and its serene fish; and the members of the family, who look like bears with a strain of hedgehog in them. Bubbies studies the pictures as I read the passage in which the little fur boy sneezes and wakes up his grandfather, who lives in a hollow stump. The grandfather appears disheveled, his eyes are dazed, and his unkempt fur is gray. Bubbies studies the drawing, then me.

The grandfather emerges from his hollow stump and says, "Bless you, my little grandson, every time you sneeze . . . Kerchoo!" The little fur child says, "Bless you," and walks on "through the dark and sunny woods." Bubbies likes the way the book begins: "There was a little fur family, warm as toast."

———◆———

The Word for the Morning is "consider." It has been selected because Jessie and Sammy have been at each other too much lately. They cannot stand it if one interrupts the other. When an adult arbitrates, deciding in favor of one of them, the other will shout, "It's not fair!" I want them to make the connection between "consider" and "considerate." I connect the two words on the Post-it at breakfast. "If 'consider' means to think about, what does 'considerate' mean?" I ask them. They do not answer. I persist. "Well, 'consider' means to think about, so who would you think about if you were being considerate?" I ask. Nothing. "If you consider something, you think about an idea or a problem. But if you are considerate, you think about . . . ?" Sammy asks, "Boppo? May we be excused?"

———◆———

Ginny and I attempt to make a dent in the stack of letters we have received—over 800 so far. Harris, Carl, Wendy, and John have received another 400, not counting emails. The letters continue to arrive from our friends, from my present and former students, from Amy's high school and college friends, from Amy's and Harris's friends, colleagues, and patients. Kate and Jim Lehrer, lifelong friends who had given their home for the funeral reception, and who have remained attentive to us since, recommended a place that prints cards of acknowledgment. I worked for Jim at the *NewsHour* for twenty-three years, and I have watched the Lehrers gracefully help others all their lives. In our free moments Ginny and I jot notes on the cards. The exercise feels like greeting a convention of all the people we have ever known, looking back on a history of friendship. Peter and Judy Weissman, our oldest friends, spent four or five weekends with us. Peter, an endocrinologist, coached Amy through organic chemistry when she was preparing for her MCATs. Other friends of ours visited on weekends as well, as did the Hales whose boys, Dylan and Ryan, are close to Jessie and Sammy. On the day Amy died, Liz and James flew down from New York and had arrived at the house before we did, even before Carl and Wendy.

My brother Peter took the train from New York. Ginny's mother, Betty, tried to make the trip but was too frail. Ginny's brothers, Lee and Ricky, came, Lee with his wife, Nancy, and their two grown children, Lee and Sarah. Reserved, good people, they stood with us stunned and brokenhearted. Sarah brought Jessie her first Webkin, a stuffed animal used in an interactive computer game. Dee, Howard, and Beth, and Rose and Bob, visited often and helped out with the children. Kindness followed upon kindness. Ginny's friends Robyn Newmyer and Kay Allaire drove her car down from Quogue so that she could use it in Bethesda. Friends phoned frequently, and send books and toys for the children. The day after Amy died, Jessie's teacher Coleen Carone came to the house and at once gathered Sammy and Jessie and seven or eight other children around her in a circle. They made paper flowers into a bouquet for Amy. Several years ago I wrote a book called *Rules for Aging*, one of which was "Nobody's thinking about you." Wrong again.

Because she paid unswerving attention to those she encountered, Amy made friends quickly—of people she met while walking the children in the neighborhood, of the nurses in the juvenile penitentiary where she had worked once a week, of Captain Ehab, who ran the car service she sometimes used, of hospital workers, of the policewoman across the road, of the saleswoman in the children's shoe department in Nordstrom's, of the Terminix man. They had crowded the funeral chapel, where the doors were left open so that those who could not get in would be able to hear the service. A hundred people had stood on the stone steps in the cold. Friends and colleagues of mine came from Stony Brook. Friends and former colleagues came from Harvard, and from *The New Republic*, the *Washington Post*, *Time*, and *The NewsHour*, where I had worked from the 1970s through the 1990s. Friends of the family came from Texas, Ohio, California, Mexico, New York, Massachusetts, Virginia, Pennsylvania, Florida, and Kentucky. One old friend flew in from Oslo. Erik Kolbell, a family friend and Congregationalist minister, who had officiated at the funeral, told the more than 500 people who attended, "What better remembrance of Amy's indistinguishable light than that we now illuminate each other's lives." John looked around and said, "I never knew we had so many friends." I said, "Neither did I."

Friendships are renewed, friendships that were strained are repaired, new friends are made. I phone Dean Anthony Grieco at the NYU School of Medicine.

Dean Grieco directs the alumni office, and is in charge of the Amy Rosenblatt Solomon Scholarship Fund. I ask him how the school plans to use the money, which, I have learned, has grown to a considerable sum with contributions from over 250 people. He tells me the fund will yield money for scholarships that will be based solely on need. Amy would approve. I tell him how grateful we are for the care shown by him and the school. Dean Grieco, who is also a professor of medicine, remembers Amy as a student. "No day goes by that I do not think of her," he says.

---

In Carl's eulogy, he noted that when people die, they are said to be in a better place. He said he did not believe that for Amy: "The best place for you [looking at the casket] is right here." He'd begun the eulogy by saying he could hear Amy telling him, "Don't screw it up."

---

The week of Amy's funeral had been difficult, but not without its distractions. At the funeral home, we were greeted by a peppy woman who asked if we wanted our car washed, an extra service. At the cemetery, we were led on a quasi–real estate tour by a woman with flaming hair who pointed out landmarks such as the headstone of a rock star who had committed suicide, and the gravesite of either the person who inspired Kermit the Frog, or Kermit himself—it was difficult to determine which. The secluded plot we chose happened to be in the Jewish section of the cemetery, admission to which, the woman informed us, was restricted to those "of Jewish blood." I assured her I had plenty. I overheard John tell Carl, "It's not a question of *if* Dad will explode, but *when*." Just as John was about to be proved right, the woman mentioned that she, too, had lost a child.

I wonder if having a religion makes death easier to take, there being established, possibly protective formalities that attend it. Ginny and I avoided religions ourselves and reared our children without one. She was born Episcopalian. We were married in a Unitarian church in New York. When we first visited the church to see if it would be right for us, they were dedicating a pew to a cat, which sealed the deal. Carl and Wendy, who was born Catholic, have a nonreligious home, as did Amy and Harris. We had something like a wake the day before the funeral, and when we greeted friends at home, it was akin to sitting shiva. But these events simply fell into place and God was not with us.

———◆———

Without looking at it, I pick up a pen to write a thank-you note for a condolence letter. I push in the button at the top of the pen, and the pen sings in a tinny voice: "Nobody's perfect. I gotta work it." Smiling at me from the barrel of the musical pink-and-purple ballpoint is Hannah Montana's irrepressible face. I get another pen.

———◆———

Few things make Jessie and Sammy happier than stories of Amy as a girl. They are interested in Amy as a teenager in New York, where we lived in the 1980s and part of the '90s. She was a very fast runner in high school. She beat Carl and John in footraces without breathing hard. And she was durable. Her brothers used to invite her to an after-dinner game called, unambiguously, "Tackle Amy." That she readily accepted their invitation was a sign of her disdain. The children are especially eager to know about their mother when she was little, like themselves. Her flagrant cuteness. When Amy turned four, Carl was so distraught at the attention she was getting in her birthday party dress, he threw himself in the garbage can.

Amy on baseball. She adopted the Kansas City Royals as her team. "I like the name," she said. "The Royals?" I asked. "Kansas City," she said. Amy watching television. One night I observed her in her transfixion as the Bionic Woman leapt over one wall and through another. "Amy," I said three or four times until she turned to me. "Amy, how does she *do* that?" The five-year-old deigned to explain, "She's bionic." Amy in peril. When she was about eight or nine months of age, and just becoming vertical, Carl used to come at her on his tricycle. Her crime was her existence. Perhaps out of a sense of fair play, he would signal his hit-and-run intentions by singing an atonal dirge that went, "Amy took the car, Amy drove it home. But she had trouble. So Carl drove . . ." As the song continued, he would barrel down on his baby sister. Upon hearing it, Ginny or I would rush to grab her up, usually before the vehicle got to her first.

Amy doing cartwheels—her preferred mode of

travel. Once, as I walked behind her, buckling under three suitcases, she cartwheeled the length of Logan Airport. Amy in kindergarten at the Sidwell Friends School in Washington, where we lived in the 1970s. Carl went there, too, and Ginny taught kindergarten and first grade there. If ever Amy caught Ginny with another child on her lap, she would saunter by and elbow her mother in the ribs as a reminder of who came first. Amy and "The Case of the Very Strange Rabbit." For her fifth birthday, we reluctantly got her a bunny that had been advertised as a "dwarf rabbit," but which grew to colossal size, nearly filling his large cage. From behind the wire mesh he stared at you with his red eyes. He was pure white. Amy named him "Raisin." Amy and Carl in competition. Amy and Carl in conspiracy. At the ages of ten and seven, they surprised Ginny with a Mother's Day breakfast in bed. They had prepared scrambled eggs without using butter in the pan, giving the dish the look and consistency of the skin of an armadillo. Smiling and chewing very slowly, Ginny ate every bite.

Boppo taking Amy shopping when she was four, for a green Lacoste dress. (Amy was pleased when I took Jessie on a similar shopping trip.) Boppo taking Amy out to dinner in a restaurant, also when she was four, just us two. She wore a blue-and-white check dress and black Mary Janes, and her hair was in bangs. We went to Billy Martin's in Georgetown. The headwaiter held Amy's chair. We sat and talked for a minute or two. Then she said she'd like to go to the ladies room. She returned to the table, but went back to the ladies room every few minutes for the duration of the meal. She didn't need to go. It made her feel sophisticated.

A favorite story of Jessie's concerns Amy when she was three, and we were living in Dunster House at Harvard. It was a Saturday morning, and I was about to go off to a meeting of a committee to award fellowships for study in Cambridge, England. At the breakfast table, I told the children it was a very old fellowship—I probably called it a prize—even older than the country, and that the boys who won the prize were very special. Three-year-old Amy was outraged. "What about the girls?" she said.

———◆———

I found it easy to beat Amy in a footrace. We would start out on a quarter-mile track, and once she had burst from the starting line and was about to leave me in the dust, I would jog some twenty yards, cut across the oval, and wait for her frown of disgust at the finish. Nothing to it.

———◆———

When Wendy was pregnant with Andrew, Ginny gave her a baby shower. She asked Amy and all the women invited to write a cherished memory of their child-hoods, which Ginny collected in a book for Wendy. Amy wrote: "One of my favorite childhood memories is when I would go out to dinner just with my Dad. I would get all dressed up and we would walk into Georgetown and go to Billy Martin's. I loved the excitement of feeling so grown up. And I loved just being with my Dad. The best part, of course, was leaving Carl at home."

———◆———

"Ginny's perfect, isn't she?" says one of our friends, observing her change Bubbies and direct Jessie to a homework assignment, while efficiently handling an "I-won't-wear-this-jacket" crisis with Sammy. "Nobody's perfect," I say, and tell him a story that makes my and

Hannah Montana's point. We were living in Cambridge. Carl was five, Amy two. It was the night before Easter and the Easter Bunny was about to pay his nocturnal visit. Carl had grown apprehensive at the prospect of an oversize egg-bearing mammal skulking about the house. At 11:00 p.m. Ginny and I were headed for bed. Carl emerged from his room and asked, "Is the Easter Bunny here yet?" No, we said, and he went back to his room. At about one a.m., he reappeared at our bedside. "Is the Easter Bunny here yet?" No, we said. "Go back to bed," said Ginny. "You'll hunt for the eggs in the morning." At 2:00 a.m., there was Carl, with the same concern. I don't think he had slept. Again at three. He stood by our bedside at 4:00 a.m. and awakened us one more time. Before he could get out his question, Ginny sat straight up and shouted, "There is no fucking Easter Bunny!" Instead of being alarmed at his mother's using a word she had probably never used before, an expression of relief washed over Carl's face. He returned to his room a happy boy.

———◆———

An Amy story I do not tell Jessie and Sammy involves the time we were moving from Cambridge to Washington. We had applied to several schools for Carl and Amy, including one with a snooty reputation in which we had little interest, but we were obliged to cover the bases. In a taxi on the way to the children's interviews at that school, Ginny and I realized we'd left Nanny, Amy's security blanket, back at the hotel. After a while, so did Amy. Nanny, in spite of having been reduced to the size of a matchbook cover, had lost none of its supernatural powers. "Where's Nanny?" said Amy. She was three and a half. I told her we'd forgotten Nanny, but not to worry. We'd talk to the people at the school and get back to Nanny as soon as possible. She took the news of our error unsympathetically, since the whole purpose of Nanny was to alleviate tense situations like that one. When we arrived for the interviews—Carl's for second grade, Amy's for kindergarten—a woman whose demeanor confirmed the school's reputation appeared and went off with the disgruntled Amy. When the interview was over, Amy looked more disgruntled, and she had trouble slipping her arms into the sleeves of her little green coat. On the way out, still battling the coat, she stomped on ahead of us down the hall, muttering but loudly, "Shit! Shit! Shit!"—language she undoubtedly had picked up from her mother. The school accepted Carl.

I teach only one writing workshop in the spring term, on the novella, so I drive to Long Island on Sunday, hold class on Monday, and return on Monday night or on Tuesday. The drive from Bethesda to Quogue feels longer than the drive back. I have mentally mapped it into segments, to help the time pass. The first and longest leg of the trip is from Bethesda to the New Jersey Turnpike, through Maryland and Delaware, which usually takes an hour and thirty-five minutes, if I don't get pulled over. From the southern end of the Turnpike to the Verrazano Bridge takes about an hour and a half. The Belt Parkway in Brooklyn takes twenty-five minutes and the Southern State Parkway, extending to eastern Long Island, another thirty-five. The last leg of the trip, consisting of the Sunrise Highway and the connecting roads to Quogue, takes about forty minutes. As one music station fades out, I pick up another, having preset the call letters for each part of the trip. Classical till the Turnpike. Jazz through New Jersey and into Brooklyn. Classical again most of the rest of the way, until the last fifteen minutes, when I listen to rock. I am learning a little about classical music as I go. I have developed a low opinion of Telemann and a high opinion of Haydn and Handel. In terms of emotions, I can take most anything but Rachmaninoff, the second symphony in particular.

Hands-free phone conversations with Carl and John, with my brother Peter, with Pete Weissman, with my longtime friend and assistant, the artist Jane Freeman, and with my Stony Brook friend and colleague Bob Reeves help speed up the drive. I check in with Ginny, who checks in with me. I try to be alert to the dangers of driving as much as I do, though sometimes I drift. Whenever I feel drowsy, I pull over and nap for a few minutes, but that rarely happens. Shirley Kenny, the president of Stony Brook, having learned of my driving schedule, wrote a letter warning me not to let my mind wander on the roadways. Ten years ago, she and her husband, Bob, lost their thirty-seven-year-old son Joel to leukemia. Her letter recalling the practical consequences of grief arrived a week after I had run a red light—the first time I'd ever done that.

I try to limit my stops to two: one at the first exit of the Turnpike, where I have a "tall" Starbucks coffee and a blueberry muffin; the other at Exit 11, to fill up. Where the Turnpike divides, I always take the lanes for cars and trucks, and not the ones for cars alone. Since I drive up on Sundays, there are few trucks and the traffic moves quickly. The lane-shift tricks of the trip have become routine. When at last I turn the corner of our street in Quogue, I am always surprised to see our house. I pull into the driveway. Entering, I turn on most of the lights.

---

Carl calls me on his cell phone nearly every morning on his way to work. I call him later in the day, and I also speak with John. Carl and John talk with each other, and with Ginny. The family always spoke frequently before Amy died, but our conversations have increased since. We seem to be assuring ourselves of the others' well-being. I have assumed the role of chief worrier, which is unlike me. Before, unless there had been a particular reason, I never worried about anything. Now the simplest casual event involving the family has me anxious. I worry when any of them takes a trip. I worry about Ginny driving in Bethesda. I worry when the children or grandchildren are down with a cold. I worry about John walking at night in New York. Ginny merely mentions a pain in her right knee. I worry.

At my urging, John arranged to have a CT angiogram, to determine that he did not have Amy's anomaly. So did Carl. The chances were minimal that either of them was at risk, but should that have been the case, there are corrective measures cardiologists can take. Because he is our youngest and on his own, I worry about John generally, trying not to show it. The more I try, the more he is aware of it. He tolerates my fretting with good humor. I ask him if he wants me to go with him to the radiologist. "Only if you buy me a toy," he says.

———◆———

Throughout the winter and the spring, there is hardly a moment for anything but play, caretaking, schooling, chauffeuring, and by 9:00 p.m., sleep. Jessie has soccer practice; Sammy has a party; Jess and Sammy have tennis; Sammy has a play-date; Jessie has Spanish; Bubbies has "gym" (an hour in which babies waddle around a large, highly polished floor, heedless of the commands of an "instructor," and bump into one another); Jessie starts piano.

When we were living in Washington, I wrote a weekly column for the *Washington Post*. One column, called "No Sleep-Overs," was a father's complaint about what was then the recent practice of overstuffing a child's day with lessons and social life. I received more hate mail in response to that piece than to anything I wrote against capital punishment or in favor of gun control. Clearly, I was out of touch, as usual.

These days, I am grateful for the children's crammed schedules. Between December and June, Sammy and Jessie had birthdays, advancing to five and seven, and Bubbies went from fourteen months to twenty. His transformation seemed like one of those time-lapse tricks in movies. In April, we celebrated Amy's birthday. When we blew out the candles, Harris asked Sammy what he thought Mommy would wish for. "To be alive," Sammy said.

He looks more like his father now, with a face that mixes independence and innocence. Jessie has perfected the ironic smile of a grown woman. When Sammy was going over the invitation list for his birthday party, which consisted of everyone in his class, he was asked if he was sure he wanted to include the class bully. "Yes," he said. "I wouldn't want him to cry." When, in a terrible coincidence, another girl's mother in Jessie's class died suddenly, Jessie said, "She can live with us."

Jessie sits at the upright piano in the little room, her back to Ginny and me. A print of lavender fields in Provence, frayed at the edges, hangs over the piano. Jessie's hair is tied with an aqua band. She wears black pants and a white shirt with long black sleeves, the front of which reads, "Color Me Happy"—every letter a different color and design. Magdalina, her young teacher, sits to her right, slightly behind her, making corrections of tempo. Jessie plays "My Robot" and "Money Can't Buy Ev'rything." "A little faster," says Magdalina quietly, with remnants of what sounds like a Russian accent. The room is one of many at the International School of Music, which sits in a small cluster of shops in Bethesda. Children come to learn the violin and clarinet and other instruments, as well as the piano. In the long hallway connecting the practice rooms, it sounds like a ragtag orchestra tuning up.

Magdalina makes checkmarks in Jessie's books as she goes along. She never interrupts. If Jessie hits a wrong note, she corrects herself. If a piece needs more practice, Magdalina tells her that. Jessie sits tall and straight. When she finishes with one of her three books, she carefully slides it into a black carrying case, and takes another. Ginny and I look at her back and watch her fingers as she plays "Bravery at Sea" and "The Happy Seal."

———————

Just before dinner on May 2, Kevin Stakey calls. He hesitates and apologizes. His voice falters. "I've come to think of you as a friend," he says.

"What is it, Kevin?"

"My son died."

His eighteen-year-old Stephen, a freshman at Stony Brook, collapsed during a mock regatta on campus. Students float cardboard boats on a pond in one of the undergraduate rites of spring.

"They don't know the cause yet," he says. "Something to do with his heart."

The next day, I drive to the North Fork of Long Island to be with Kevin and his family, whom I have not met. His pretty wife, Cathy, is blond, with a wide and open face and the look of someone who gets things done—the adult version of their fourteen-year-old daughter, Laura. Laura greets me politely, so does nine-year-old Andrew. Cathy calls me "Mr. Rosenblatt," until I ask her not to. We sit in the brightly lit and spotless living room of the gray, two-story house that Kevin built, and they tell me about Stephen—how easily he made friends, how he loved playing the bass drum in the university band. He had been valedictorian of his Mattituck High School class. Every few minutes Cathy offers me something to eat. I recognize this improbable impulse to play host to those who grieve with you. Kevin's dad comes by. He is a huge man, well over six feet and larger than Kevin. He sits with us, says nothing, and eventually takes Andrew for a walk.

Before returning to Bethesda, I tell Kevin not to concern himself with whatever remains to be done on the playhouse. Two days later, he is back at work.

———————

Ginny has a choking fit at breakfast. It lasts only seconds, but Jessie freezes. Sammy runs from the room.

———————

On the last day of Sammy's pre-school, the Geneva Day School dedicated a bench to Amy's memory. Jessie had gone to Geneva two years earlier, and next year would be Bubbies's turn. The bench was Leslie Adelman's and Laura Gwyn's idea, and the teachers and families of the school contributed. Leslie had a landscaper plant bushes and tulips behind the bench, and Jim Bryla, the contractor who had redone Amy's and Harris's deck and basement, installed it. When Jim and his crew were working on the house, Amy had stocked a refrigerator with soft drinks and made lunches for them. The bench was made of teak, and three circles were carved into the back, to represent the three children. It also bore a small bronze plaque, donated by a school parent, that read "In loving memory of Amy Solomon, mother of Jessica, Sammy and James." The bench was placed near a fence at the center of the playground, so that parents could sit and enjoy the sight of their children playing.

The ceremony was held at noon on a bright, hot day at the end of May, the Friday of Memorial Day weekend. After the dedication of the bench, there would be a closing-day carnival and a picnic. Some seventy-five people gathered in a circle. Speakers included Sammy's teacher, Ed Bullis, an upbeat young man who entertains the kids with his singing, and who has kept a careful eye on Sammy since Amy's death. He calls Sammy "Samalama." Mrs. Funk, the head of Geneva, who also spoke, handed out watering cans to the family for the flowers around Amy's bench. Jessie, Sammy, and Bubbies watered the tulips. Mrs. Funk and Mr. Bullis spoke of Amy being a part of the school, and of seeing her on the playground, involved with her own children and others.

Carl spoke and Harris spoke. Harris told of how much being a mom meant to Amy, that it was her life's priority. She was very serious about being a doctor, and practiced medicine to be of use, he said, but she had turned down equity and a partnership to be more of a full-time mother. Leslie spoke. She said, "The night before Amy died, I was with her at her home. I noticed that a candle I had given her when James turned one was still sitting next to her phone in the kitchen—months later. She told me that she loved the smell of the candle and kept it there so that she could enjoy it in the midst of life's craziness. We joked about the fact that she could not find the time to actually light the candle." She said Amy never regretted that, or anything she did not have or did not do. "To Amy, life was never about more."

When the ceremony was finished, no one would go

near the bench, as if it were sanctified. Then a father casually went over with his child. They sat and ate sandwiches.

———◆———

On July Fourth weekend, the family comes to Quogue, as it does every year, to celebrate Carl's birthday on the second. This year, not only do Carl and Wendy bring Andrew and Ryan to join their cousins, but we also ask Scott Huber, Wendy's brother, and Risa, and their two girls, Sydney and Caitlin, whom Jessie and Sammy also call cousins. Somewhere residing in our house are seven children under the age of six, and eight adults, including John. There is one brief meltdown, Jessie's, which we ought to have anticipated when she grew aware of all the mothers present but her own. "It's not fair!" she cried. Harris sat with her in what served as a children's dormitory. She said, "I want the cousins." Carl came in with the rest of the kids, and suggested that they all jump from bed to bed. Jessie led the pack.

Jessie disapproves of my association with three-year-old Caitlin Huber. A while back, Caitlin recognized a fellow loner in me, and chose me as her playmate. Her idea of play is to order me around. She gives me coloring books and tells me to stay within the lines. When she was first being potty-trained, she told her mother that I was to empty out the potty chair. Jessie observed our relationship without comment until this weekend, when she saw that I had brought a Kleenex box with a picture of a princess on it. She told Ginny, "Boppo probably got that for Caitlin."

Scott and Risa, both doctors, got along very well with Amy and Harris, as they do with Carl and Wendy and John. Until Amy died, I had acknowledged them as extended family, but did not make an effort to know them as individuals. Now I feel the need to do that, and to know Risa's two sisters, Jayme and Allison, as well, and their husbands, Michael and Ray, and Risa's parents, Chuck and Ilene, who always went out of their way for Amy. On the weekend, the children ride bikes and play in the pool, for which I got an inflatable crocodile with an arresting leer. Bubbies drives his red Cozy Coupe, and "cooks" hotdogs on his toy stove. We sing "Happy Birthday" to Carl.

Our bedroom doubles as a gallery for family photographs—Carl and Wendy on their wedding day, Amy and Harris on theirs. There is a picture of me and Andrew at the piano; of all five grandchildren in various coerced poses; one of John in gown and mortarboard at his college graduation; two of Amy and Ginny, their heads close together, looking like sisters. In one picture, Jessie and I are on the beach in Quogue. In another, Amy and I are on a beach in Cape Cod. She is Jessie's age, has a towel around her shoulders, and looks cold from the water. A picture of Amy in a blue baseball cap holding Bubbies. A picture of Amy holding Sammy on her hip, she smiling, he looking curious. A full-faced, charismatic picture of Bubbies, a few months old; and of Amy at the age of two, either putting on or removing Ginny's sunglasses. The photos are distributed on the walls, on Ginny's desk, on the mantelpiece, the bed tables, the dresser.

Once in a while, Ginny is brought down by the sight of them, or of any artifact connected to a memory. I am more often felled by mundane problems or momentary concerns, such as choosing a shirt to wear or remembering to take a pill—since nothing will ever be normal again. On the beige carpet at the foot of the dresser there is a small rust-colored stain. It had happened on the afternoon of December 8, shortly after Ginny and I received Carl's call about Amy. We were packing hurriedly to leave for Bethesda, and in trying to screw the cap on a bottle of baby aspirin, I spilled the pills. I picked them up weeks later, and they left a stain.

———————◆———————

We have always liked Quogue for the tone it sets and preserves—private people going about quiet lives. Several friends from the village made the trip to Amy's funeral, including Susie and Denny Lewis. Their son Denny was killed in Argentina, between college and medical school. He was riding in a car driven by a reckless, speeding driver. There were letters from dozens more, many of whom had never met Amy and who barely knew us. Charlie and Anne Mott called often. Their son-in-law, Marc Reisner, died of appendiceal cancer in 2000. Anne and Charlie have helped their daughter, Lawrie, with their two granddaughters. Andrew Botsford wrote a moving obituary of Amy in the *Southampton Press*, where he is associate editor. Christine Clifton and her staff at the Quogue Library sent a plant. Aurora Jones of Flowers by Rori knew Amy from the time she provided roses for her wedding. She greeted us in tears on our return, as did Lulie Morrisey, another friend who embraced us in the post office. Amy used to fast-walk to the Quogue Country Market for her morning coffee, pushing first Jessie, then Sammy, then Bubbies in the stroller ahead of her. She chatted with the owners, Bob and Gary, and with the people behind the counter—Sue, Gerard, Lisa, and the woman we referred to as our "other Ginny." They were steeped in grief. Ginny, who has worked at the market many years, wrote a tender note, and little Sue came out from behind the counter to hug us, her head bowed, without saying a word.

It was Amy who brought us to Quogue in the first place. We had spent parts of two summers renting in East Hampton and in Bridgehampton, where the relentless social life was getting to us. Amy, a college sophomore, was working as a short-order cook in a tennis club in Quogue, serving burgers and sandwiches. She knew that Ginny and I were tired of the Hamptons and were talking of spending future summers elsewhere, perhaps in New England. "Before you decide," she said, "you ought to take a look at Quogue. It's like you"—meaning boring.

"I can still see her at the table in the kitchen," Ginny said to me over the weekend. "All those physics and chemistry books."

Amy was catching up with the preparatory courses for medical school. She had taken not a single science course in college, and had only decided on medicine after two years of waitressing and bartending and thinking she might become an actor. We asked an actor friend if he would speak to her about the requirements and pitfalls of the profession. Amy emerged from the two-hour conversation intent on becoming a doctor. We told our friend that if he gave his mini-lecture to every young person aspiring to be an actor, parents would pay him a fortune.

I wish my dad had lived long enough to see her start out in her practice. We gave Amy his medical bag as a gift for her medical school graduation. On one side of the bag, just below the handles, were my father's initials in gold letters. We had Amy's initials put on the other side. When we presented her with the bag, she held it close and sighed, "Oh."

---

In 1996, I wrote an essay on the character of physicians for *New York* magazine's issue on the city's "Best Doctors." Amy was in her second year of medical school, and

I interviewed her for the piece. I asked her how medicine had changed from my dad's era to hers. She said that formerly physicians had stature and mystery. Her grandfather "was a *Doctor*," she said. "I'll just be a doctor."

"Why hasn't the stature of doctors risen, given all that medicine has accomplished in the past few years?" I asked her.

"It's odd," she said. "Doctors used to be the be- and end-all when they knew very little. Now that they know so much more, it works to their disadvantage. When something goes wrong, people think: 'Well, they should have known,' and the fact that the ordinary person knows so much about medicine demystifies the profession. The idea of a second opinion is sound practice now. Yet it seems to imply that the first opinion is likely to be wrong. And then, too, death may have been more generally accepted years ago. People don't believe in death these days. But doctors do."

"Is it more of a job than a calling?" I said.

"More of a job, but an interesting job," she said. "If I were viewing it as a calling, I think I'd be disappointed. But the work itself is endlessly fascinating. The driving force for doctors is simply not knowing."

Moments of "not knowing" could also have painful consequences. I remember my father's drained and helpless face when a patient he had been treating for a long time died of lung cancer, my father's specialty. I remember Amy's face a few years ago after the death of a patient, a one-and-a-half-year-old child. He had been born prematurely with multiple developmental problems related to hydrocephalus. A ventricular-peritoneal shunt had been placed in his brain to release pressure by draining increased fluid to his abdomen. The child had been neglected by his mother, but his foster mother, whom Amy respected, had been diligent about checkups. An infection developed in the shunt. The symptoms were barely detectable, as is usual with developmentally delayed babies. Still, Amy felt she should have noticed some small sign of change. Doctors often depend on an educated sixth sense about trouble, since most of the time they deal with commonplace ailments. A pediatrician mainly sees breaks, sores, bruises, cuts, colds, and strep. Harris told me, "She took it very hard when the child died. She had a great sixth sense, but she thought it had failed her. She blamed herself."

All Amy wanted out of medicine, as she said in the interview for the *New York* magazine piece, was "to make people feel better." Her friend Liz Hale, a dermatologist, told me, "In part of a single evening, Amy taught me more about nursing a screaming baby than all the lactation professionals I consulted." Her pediatric colleague, Gail Warner, said, "Most doctors are smart, but Amy had judgment, too. I used to go to her with *my* problems." She also appreciated the wonder within the science of her work. When Andrew had just been born, and we all were in the hospital room with Wendy, Amy picked up the new baby, flipped him over, turned him this way and that, and studied him like a photographer holding a negative to the light.

———◆———

Amy is responsible for getting my toaster in Quogue. It replaced a toaster that no one but me could stand because you had to find the precise setting or it would burn the toast, or undercook it, or toast only one side of the bread. Amy hated that toaster more than anyone because of the toll it took on bagels. I defended it, mainly for its Art Deco look. It was streamlined, chrome, and round at the edges. But Amy favored reality over appearance, and when planning a gift for my birthday, she persuaded Harris, Carl, Wendy, and John that they should pool their resources and get me a new expensive Viking "professional" toaster that worked. It has a "warm" feature on the dial, and a boxier shape than the old toaster, which I keep around as a backup. The old one also serves as an auxiliary toaster, when I have to accommodate all the children at once. But the new one is my best toaster.

———◆———

After the July Fourth weekend, Ginny, Harris, and the children return to Maryland. Jessie and Sammy are eager to get back to their Wii, a virtual reality video game that Harris got them at the start of the summer. I need to stay on in Quogue for the Southampton Writers Conference, which extends from mid-July to the end of the month. The writers, who also teach workshops, pair up for the evening readings. This summer I am partnered with Frank McCourt. Frank reads from his first work of fiction. I had thought to read from my novel *Beet*, which had come out in February. But while looking for something in a tangle of papers, I came across an essay I'd written for *Time* twenty-one years earlier, called "Speech for a High School Graduate." It was an attempt at a literary commencement speech, written to honor Amy. I wrote similar *Time* essays for Carl and John upon their high school graduations, using the trope of a father giving his personal commencement speech to his children as he looked to their future.

I decide to read the essay instead of the passage from my novel. I would not have done so for an audience of strangers, but Bob Reeves, the conference director, has fostered a familial atmosphere over the years, and the participants have grown close. When Amy died, Billy Collins wrote us, "Sometimes there *are* no words." Frank, Matt Klam, Lou Ann Walker, Meg Wolitzer, and others stayed in constant touch. Melissa Bank sent a little package containing a floral handkerchief for Ginny, audiotapes of short stories for my drives, and a chestnut she had found in the driveway of a restaurant in Tuscany some years ago, which had given her comfort. I do not think the essay to Amy will feel inappropriate. So after Frank finishes, I read what I had written when Amy was seventeen. It interests me how many of my wishes for her had come true—her love of travel, of animals, of music, her appreciation of history, her enthusiasm for sports, her respect for traditions. I wished her fierceness in battle, but urged her not to hang onto corrosive enmities. I wished her a love of work, predicting that it would have "something to do with helping others." I wished her productive solitudes, and worthy friends, though in her case that wish was superfluous. I wished her the pleasure of an exchange of wit with a stranger, and moments of helpless hilarity. I wished her life in a place where she might see a stretch of sky. The essay ends with a promise never to let go.

---

Ginny comes back for the opening of the conference. Soon she will have to return to Bethesda, where Jessie and Sammy have begun camp for the rest of the month, but for an unusual couple of days we have each other's company. At dusk we take a walk. We feel older and smaller than we do with the grandchildren. The sky is orange and pink, the streets vacant except for the sounds of children in their houses. We speak of the presidential campaign and of things in the news.

On evenings in previous summers we would walk to the ocean, half a mile from our house. Or we would go only as far as the bridge over the Shinnecock Canal, and turn back. Tonight we stay on the streets that run like tributaries to the water. We are familiar with these

old and confident houses, though not with all their oc-
cupants. We know some houses intimately, since we
traipsed through them when they were up for sale. Our
house was out of reach when it was first on the market,
but the owners had three homes elsewhere, and eventually accepted our offer, which terrified us. We walk over
to Penniman's Creek, where the water rummages with
the pebbles.

"I'm thinking of getting a kayak," I tell her.

"Do you know how to use a kayak?" she says.

"I've done it two or three times."

"Is it dangerous?" she says.

"No. I'll get one for you, too."

"I think I'd be scared," she says.

I tell her, "If I can do it, anybody can do it."

It is nearly dark, and the streets have gone from
gray to black. We hear the pop-pop of tennis balls. We
hold hands, the way we did when we first dated in high
school. I make a mental note to call a place in Wainscott
that sells kayaks.

On Quogue Street, we pass the home of our friend
and next-door neighbor, Ambrose Carr, whose wife,
Nancy, a kind and beautiful woman, died the November
before last. She had been ill for a long while. Amby, a

little older than we, has a patrician voice and the face of a 1930s leading man. One morning we chatted in the post office. In the early afternoon, he walked over from his yard to ours to tell me Nancy had just died in her sleep. When Amy died, he left a phone message for Ginny and me: "I love you." These days he travels a bit, visits his children and grandchildren, tends his garden, and listens to jazz.

———◆———

In Bethesda, Ginny writes a poem called "Arch of Shade"—

> Rachmaninoff and Mozart
> Sift through the haze
> On River Road.
> Two hatted women wait
> In the heat for the Ride-on-bus.
> The Wii is the summer wish
> Come true.
> Your babies' crib is disassembled
> And taken away
> Accepted

With gratitude
To be the bed for a new life.

I am turning
To the camp carpool line
Only thinking of you.
The arch of shade hovers
The hot July sun rays
Dapple the leaf arch
To highlight the darkness.

I am here.

---

Ginny began writing poems three years ago, and has published a couple of them. They are very much like her. Nearly all begin with the description of a pleasant scene, often bucolic, then pivot toward the expression of a more serious idea or feeling. It is as if she were welcoming you into the poem, and when you walk in and feel at ease, she closes the door behind you, to reveal her real purpose, which, in "Arch of Shade" is to "highlight the darkness." You must go back up the lines to detect earlier hints of that purpose, such as the women waiting in the heat and the disassembled crib. You might say, "I didn't see that coming," but the signs were there. So it is with Ginny. Her graciousness distracts people from noticing that she is alert to life's dark places. She prefers it that way. Her poems hit their mark but gently. They crack the egg without breaking it.

---

All five grandchildren come to Quogue for most of the month of August—Jessie, Sammy, Bubbies, Andrew, and Ryan. Ligaya comes too, guaranteeing our survival. In two shifts, the children arrive late at night, and they run from the cars to the playhouse. They have already declared it "awesome."

Kevin has built us a small stage, and one of the children's early productions is a reenactment of *American Idol*. I play Paula. Another is a play based on Sammy's imagined utopia of Moseybane. We call it "The King of Moseybane." Harris had ordered costumes online for Sammy (the King); Ryan (the Prince); Jessie (the Wizard); and Andrew (the Knight). Boppo (the Dragon) and Bubbies (the Narrator) require no costumes.

On opening night (which coincides with closing night), Ryan appears onstage with his mother, Wendy. Andrew would not appear at all at first, but, when coaxed, delivers his lines from memory. Jessie's over-the-top Wizard is indistinguishable from her *American Idol* audition. The King looks stunned with his own power. Bubbies decides that his one line, "Dookies"—his word for his favorite cookie—will be more effective if delivered from the driveway, fifty feet from the stage, with Harris beside him. The Dragon has to compromise his ferocity by reading all the parts, except Jessie's and Andrew's. In spite of these creative differences, the audience—my brother Peter, Bob and Beth Reeves, and the remaining family grown-ups—is appreciative. The bewildered cast receives a standing ovation.

---

Before the summer, I got Obama baseball caps for Ginny, Harris, Carl, Wendy, John, the five grandchildren, and myself. I had the caps made to order in a specialty store in the Tyson's Corner, Virginia, shopping mall. White caps with "Obama" in navy blue lettering—very handsome caps. In a brief if overblown ceremony, I presented

everyone with a one-of-a-kind Obama cap. Harris said it
would make him look silly to his medical partners. John
simply said it would make him look silly. Carl said no
one in the company he works for knew who Obama was.
Wendy looked mildly pleased. Each of the children tried
the cap on for approximately half a second, then tossed
it aside, never to pick it up again. I wore mine often.
Ginny, who had been running a one-woman campaign
for Obama for the past two years, wore hers everywhere.
Distracted by the children, she left it on the beach one
day. The following afternoon—though the cap did not
have her name in it—the lifeguard returned it to her.
Amy would have looked great in that cap, her pony tail
bouncing out of the opening in the back.

———◆———

Wendy announces to the family that she is pregnant.
Jessie hopes it's a girl.

———◆———

With two additional customers, I become a short-order
cook, on the receiving end of commands fired at me all

at once: cereal, no cereal; cereal with milk and without; orders for skim milk added to Silk and "cow milk"; minipancakes and miniwaffles, with and without sugar, with and without butter, with and without syrup. Bubbies remains consistent in his preference for toast.

To deliberately irk Sammy, I teach Andrew and Ryan the "Boppo National Anthem." At once Ryan adopts it as his favorite song (I do not know how many other songs he knows), and he sings it at the top of his quite considerable voice. Andrew seems to tolerate the anthem, but is skeptical of the lyrics. He wants to know if I am truly great. I look at Sammy who smiles with derision. By now, Bubbies is old enough to pick up the song. Jessie, always a good sport, goes along, so the morning glee club consists of the boisterous baritone of Ryan, the hesitant tenor of Andrew, the forceful soprano of Jessie, the raspy alto of Bubbies, and Sammy, belting, "I hope he's not stinky." It occurs to me that the other adults may not approve of this exercise in self-aggrandizement, but that is the price one pays when one is truly great.

My anger, being futile, flares in the wrong places and at the wrong times. One evening I blew up at three-year-old Ryan. Ryan not only has size and a deep voice, he also has a gangster's way of speaking, which amuses everyone, Carl and Wendy especially. When he wants water, he growls, "Waw-duh!" He had just run headlong into Bubbies, flattening him in the hall upstairs. I yelled and Ryan cowered. He grabbed his binky. I took it away from him. I overreacted. I apologized. He apologized. He said, "I wish I had super powers so I could fly over Bubbies and not hit him."

Wendy was sore at me for coming down on Ryan as hard as I did. She was silently sore, doubling my guilt. Wendy is dear to me, and she is careful and loving with Jessie, Sammy, and Bubs. She understands that women like herself, and Liz Hale, Leslie Adelman, and a few others of Amy's age, represent a connection to Amy. The children may look at these women, remember how their mother was with them, and see them as surrogates. I know they do that with Aunt Wendy. I promised myself I'd make things right with her, but I didn't have to. Soon after my blunder with Ryan, we were good again without my having to try.

———◆———

Amy and Harris were married in our Quogue house in 1998 on one of those fiercely bright June days which draw artists to eastern Long Island. It never mattered to Amy that we could not afford a big wedding like those of her friends. I told her what was possible. She was thrilled. We rented a big white tent, which billowed in the wind on the front lawn. Amy and Harris chose a band from New York that played mostly sixties music. There were blue blazers and red ties and navy-blue dresses with white trim, and many white roses. The sky was clear as glass.

We had asked Amy what sort of ceremony she and Harris wanted, and she said they'd like the cartoonist Garry Trudeau, a close family friend, to marry them. After making inquiries, we learned that New York State does not permit cartoonists (or any other layperson, for that matter) to perform wedding ceremonies, so we arranged for two ceremonies—one by the cartoonist and a legal one performed by Erik Kolbell. The morning of the wedding, Amy, Ginny, and Jane Pauley, the television journalist and Garry's wife, were having their hair done at the Quogue beauty parlor. Jane had given Amy a pair of diamond earrings to wear as "something borrowed." At the beauty parlor she told Amy her earrings would be borrowed only until the pronouncement of man and wife, after which they would be hers to keep. Garry said many beautiful things to the couple, before telling the assembled that he was marrying Amy and Harris with the power vested in him "by the State of Euphoria."

The following day, before Amy and Harris went off on their honeymoon, we served a brunch for the wedding party and friends. Amy and I took a walk, just the two of us, arms around each other. I do not recall what we said.

———◆———

Bubbies sits in my lap in the den. He locks his hands behind his head when he relaxes. I do the same. We sit there in a lopsided brown leather chair—same pose, sitting in tandem, like luge drivers.

One evening, he points to the shelf to his left and says, "Book." He indicates *The Letters of James Joyce*, edited by Stuart Gilbert. It seems an ambitious choice for a twenty-three-month-old boy, but I take down the book and prop it up before us.

"Dear Bubbies," I begin. "I went to the beach today, and played in the sand. I also built a castle. I hope you will come play with me soon. Love, James Joyce."

Bubbies seems content, so I "read" another:

*"Dear Bubbies,*

*Went to the playground today. Tried the slide. It was a little scary. I like the swings better. I can go very high, just like you.*

*Love,*

*James Joyce."*

Bubbies turns the pages. I occasionally amuse myself with an invented letter closer to the truth of Joyce's life and personality.

*"Dear Bubbies,*

*I hate the Catholic Church, and am leaving Ireland forever.*

*Love,*

*James Joyce."*

It tickles me that Bubbies has chosen to latch onto a writer who gladly would have stepped on a baby to get a rave review.

I try to put back the book, but he detects an implicit

announcement of his bedtime, and he protests. "Joyce!" he says. Eventually, he resigns himself to the end of his day. He puts the book back himself, and quietly says, "Joyce."

---

When Bubbies was a few months old, Amy used to prop him on her knees, hold him under the arms, and look straight into his eyes with an indefinite urgency. Then she would sing her curious lyrics to the tune of "Frère Jacques," which now makes me wonder if she had an unconscious premonition that she would not be around for him.

> *We are the strong men, we are the strong men.*
> *We lift weights, we lift weights.*
> *Heavy weights and light weights,*
> *Heavy weights and light weights.*
> *We are the strong men.*

---

I drive Ginny and Jessie to New York, and join them for a pancakes-and-French-toast breakfast at a diner uptown, then go my own way. This is to be a girls' day out in the big city. Sammy will have his own day later on. In the morning Ginny and Jessie go to a hair salon, where Jessie gets a blow-dry and has her nails polished. The manicurist asks what color she wants. She chooses an electric blue.

In the early afternoon they go to the American Girl store, a mecca for preteens in midtown, on Fifth Avenue. The store sells the American Girl dolls and their clothing and paraphernalia, clothes for children to dress like their dolls, books about dolls, paper dolls, has a tearoom where a child can have lunch or tea with her doll (it is booked solid, so Ginny and Jess lunch elsewhere), and a doll hospital. Jessie gets an American Girl sweatshirt and a white nightgown for herself and her doll, and two books. She also buys a computer game for her friend Oana.

They stroll and they chat, taking in the still magnitude of New York on an August day. They go downtown to the West 20s, where friends of ours, the artist David Levinthal, his wife, Kate Sullivan, and their little boy, Sam, live in a large loft. Kate is a professional baker. She and Jess make cookies together in various shapes, and she gives Jessie molds to make more. On the way back uptown, Ginny points out the Gramercy Park neighborhood where I had grown up, and where she and I spent lots of time in our high school and college years. John ends his workday with us at dinner. John has always been a favorite with the children, who are drawn to his gentleness and reserve. At his appearance, Jessie cheers. She deems the day "perfect."

———◆———

Carl, Wendy, and the boys return to Fairfax, leaving Ginny, Harris, the children, and me to spend a few days together before summer ends. I stand holding Jessie's hand at the lip of the ocean. When she was a baby, she would not allow her feet to touch the sand. Sammy had the same reaction to snow. Neither child trusted uncertain surfaces. Now Jessie plunges into the water. Harris sits a few yards away making a castle with a moat with Sammy. Ginny wears her Obama cap. She and Bubbies remain under the yellow-and-white-striped umbrella. She reads to him, her calm and patience limitless.

A picture comes to mind of my mother reading to Peter when he was Bubbies's age. She too was a teacher. I watched them as they sat on lawn chairs in a hotel where we were staying, my mother positioning the book under a shaft of sunlight.

I tell Jessie, "Here comes the wave. Here it goes. Will it touch our knees or our ankles or our toes?"

"Our toes," she says.

Miles east of here, the beaches of Southampton and East Hampton are mobbed, but in Quogue the beach lies open, with ample room for play and for walking. A girl about Jessie's age approaches and introduces herself. "I'm Schuyler," she says. Jessie greets her warmly. She moves on. Jessie watches the boats against the pale sky. She watches the bigger boys on their boogie boards. She smiles with her mouth slightly open and gap-toothed and amazed, the way Amy did at her age.

"Let's go in!" says Harris. He and I take turns holding Jessie in the waves. She swims from one of us to the other as we tread water about thirty feet apart. Ginny, on shore with the boys, observes us anxiously. A strong swimmer, she has always been wary of the ocean. Amy was also a strong swimmer. Our favorite photo of her as a six-year-old was taken in a swimming pool in Washington, Amy underwater, doing the breaststroke toward the camera.

"Daddy! Here I come!"

Before heading home, we get ice cream cones. Sammy wants a sugar cone with vanilla ice cream and rainbow sprinkles. Jess and Bubbies want cups of vanilla. Harris abstains. Ginny and I have moosetracks. Constellations of families are spread out on the beach. Ours does not look very different from the others.

---

Late in August, we return to Bethesda for the first days of the children's schools. Bubbies begins preschool at Geneva. Ginny takes him. He cries on his first day, and is fine after that. School for someone thirty inches high—it seems preposterous. Jessie starts second grade at Burning Tree, Sammy kindergarten. He is excited, mainly about taking the school bus. The first day, Sammy's bus runs out of oil on the way home.

"What was your favorite part of the day?" I ask him.

"When the school bus couldn't move," he says. Harris says that might turn out to be Sammy's favorite part of the whole year.

On the weekend, we visit the cemetery. Each time, I go with a mixture of need and trepidation, because I know I may break down at the sight of the small rectangle of earth, the boxwood outlining it, the conical brass receptacle for flowers, and the marker, which is so definite. When we chose this spot in December, the nearby office buildings showed through the shorn trees. Since spring the area has burgeoned with dogwoods and magnolias.

Jessie has brought white carnations; Sammy, a Washington Redskins balloon in the shape of an oversized football, which he plans to release into the air. He seems fragile these days—drifting into faraway stares and silences. Yet he talks more about Amy's death. Yesterday morning, he asked me again how Mommy died. "The heart stopped. Right?" he said. His first day of kindergarten, when the children were asked to draw pictures of their families, Sammy's drawing included Amy lying dead on the floor. Catherine Andrews, the children's psychotherapist, says that Sammy is expressing recollections as they come to him, but that this is a way of expelling them, and they are unlikely to be repeated.

At the gravesite, Harris asks Sammy if he has something to say. He stands behind the marker and says, "I miss you, Mommy." He tells Amy about Bubbies's first teacher in preschool, Ms. Franzetti, and about Jessie's second-grade teacher, Mrs. Salcetti, and about his own, Ms. Merritt. He tells Amy about the balloon, and predicts the Redskins will win the Superbowl. Jessie has no message for Amy today. Sammy asks Harris if he can be buried next to Mommy. Harris says yes, but tells him it's a very long way off.

Ginny and I take turns holding Bubbies, who carries a small plastic penguin. When you squeeze its "trigger," its beak opens and shuts, its little wings flap, and the penguin squawks. On an earlier visit to the cemetery, Bubbies refused to be taken from his car seat, and cried out, "No, no, no!" Today he has his penguin, and is content simply to look around.

Jessie places the carnations in the conical vessel. Harris writes, "We love you, Mommy" on the football balloon. The children let it go. It flies up in the heavy air and snags on a distant tree. We assure the children that the wind will free it eventually.

---

Bubbies's birthday is in September, so is mine. For his, we gathered Carl, Wendy, and their boys, made a to-do, and gave him a toy grill to further his culinary bent.

"How old are you, Bubs?" I asked him. "Two!" he said. For my birthday, Ginny gave me the kayak. Harris gave me an imitation Andy Warhol, which he ordered up on the Internet. It consists of four versions of a picture of Bubbies and me in Disney World last January, me leaning back on a bench, Bubbies standing behind it pulling my hair. In each picture, the hair, eyes, and skin are different colors. Ginny and I hung it in our bedroom where Bubbies likes to look at himself with green hair and me with blue. He comes down to the room all the time, to steal and hide Ginny's curlers, or try to take my car keys, or to ask, "What is that?" about everything. Our room has become a home, with places for books, shoes, and suitcases, pictures of Amy and the grandchildren on my desk, and the kids bouncing in and out. Sammy will watch TV on our bed when Jessie has commandeered the one upstairs. Jessie wants to know how my IBM Selectric typewriter works. It fascinates her to see me at it—one antique using another.

One evening, Sammy rushes into the room naked from head to toe. "Boppo!" he says, having just watched a DVD of *101 Dalmatians*. "The dalmatian puppies were saved!" I ask, "Sammy, where are your clothes?" He says, "The puppies were going to be skinned for coats!"

He glances at Amy's picture. "I miss Mommy," he says. "Me, too," I say.

———◆———

To the array of the children's activities have been added martial arts for Sammy, a new gym with balance beams and monkey bars for Bubbies, and yoga for Jess. On Saturday mornings in the fall, she has soccer. Her team, the Flames, wears uniforms of blazing yellow. Games are played simultaneously on three adjacent fields. Rob Hazan, the Flames' coach, is married to Jill, a high school friend of Harris's. Jill and the other mothers sit together on collapsible canvas chairs in the cool fall air, and Ginny sits with them.

This is the way it was when our children were small—parents loosely convened for recitals, plays, pageants, basketball, Little League. In Vermont, where we rusticated for a year between my jobs at the *Washington Post* and at *Time* in New York, we cheered in the bleachers of drafty school gyms with John in his stroller, as Carl hit a winning jump shot in a local basketball tournament and Amy scored all her team's points in an elementary school game—four. In Bethesda it is as Ginny noted: she is leading Amy's life. With one mother, she makes plans for a trip to the National Zoo; with another, a date to see *Madagascar.* The women speak of their children's teachers. They praise, they complain, they collaborate, they gossip.

On Halloween, we go to the Burning Tree School to admire Sammy, Jessie, and the other children in their costumes and to watch a parade. Jessie's second-grade teacher, Deirdre Salcetti, is a creative, quick-witted blonde in her forties, with a you're-safe-with-me smile, which readily surrenders to laughter. She has the body of a gymnast. She teaches the yoga classes. Dressed as a bee today, she has antennas on her head and wears translucent wings and a tag that reads, "Don't worry. Bee happy." Mrs. Salcetti stands before the class. "I'm not going to start until everyone is quiet." The children prepare to present themselves to the visitors.

A girl steps forward as Indiana Jones, and explains who she is. Another girl appears as one of the Jedi. Katie, who has no hair, is a wizard. I surmise that she is being treated for cancer, but am told that she has a genetic disorder. Her face is startlingly white. She smiles readily. A girl named Amy is a witch with a cat and a broom.

"Will you be riding your broom later?" asks Mrs. Salcetti.

"I'm a good witch," says Amy.

Here comes Dorothy, carrying Toto in a basket and wearing glittery red shoes. She clicks her heels three times. Here is Michael, the Incredible Hulk. Jaraad is an alien with a green face. Others arrive: a Tootsie Roll, an Eloise, an Uncle Sam, a Bride of Frankenstein with a white stripe in her hair. "I really need to see better with this helmet on," says another *Star Wars* character. I ask a boy in an Obama mask, "Are you running for President?" He says, "No." Jessie appears. Confident and forceful, she announces she's a Power Ranger.

The parents and Ginny and I are asked to proceed outside for the Halloween parade. We pass signs, mottos, and aphorisms of encouragement on the school walls. A painted dog balances a ball on its nose over the words, "No one can do everything, but everyone can do something." I greet Andrew, an autistic boy who was in Jessie's first-grade class last year. He had a special teacher to help him. He used to ask me, "Are you my Daddy?" I cannot determine if he recognizes me, but he gives me a hug.

Sammy's kindergarten class is lined up in the hall,

shepherded by Pam Merritt. Ms. Merritt has the independent, high-style look of the favorite aunt, regal posture, a blues-singer's smoky voice, and wears red sneakers. Sammy is Ironman, his new number-one superhero. He sees us and waves.

Gypsies, angels, Spidermen, Supermen. They file past the crowd and kick up the fallen leaves. Harris, who has taken off early from work, joins us. Jessie and Sammy march by and light up at the sight of him. Fathers and mothers step out of the pack to take pictures. Children pose before the red-brick wall or under the trees of muted autumn colors. At the appearance of a girl dressed as Sherlock Holmes, Ginny and I exchange a look. One Halloween, when Carl was eight and Amy five, they had a battle royal over who would dress as Sherlock Holmes and who as Dr. Watson. Carl said, "I'm the oldest, so I'm Holmes." Amy said, "Dr. Watson was the oldest, too. You're Watson." They each dressed as Holmes, referring to the other as an imposter.

---

Bubbies sings and dances to "Toddler Favorites." Ginny leads him: "Where is Thumbkin, where is Thumbkin?"

They sing, "Here I am, here I am." Ginny employs the unnervingly precise voice of the former schoolteacher. She knows all the hand gestures that accompany the lyrics. "Here I am." She holds her thumbs in front of her. "How are you today, sir? Very well, I thank you." She wiggles her thumbs as if they are talking to each other. "Run away. Run away." She hides her thumbs behind her back. Bubbies is mesmerized, as am I.

"How do you know to do that stuff?" I ask.

"I'm programmed," she says. "Scary, isn't it?"

———◆———

I tend to do whatever Bubbies says, but Harris talks to him as if he were in his midtwenties. (He also has taken to calling him James now that he is in school, and with some resistance, I generally go along.) One Sunday morning, before I packed to get ready for my drive to Quogue, James was in his usual place at the kitchen table, telling people where he wanted them to sit. He does that. If you take a seat he does not sanction, he will shake a fist at you. "Sit here"—some other place. Only he seems to know the proper assignments. That morning Ginny had taken the wrong seat, so James let her have it.

"Mimi sit here!"—indicating the other side of the table. Harris entered and told him, "Don't worry about where people sit." The offhand tone of Harris's command had me laughing for much of my drive. I called Harris from Quogue at the end of the afternoon. "Do you realize," I said, "that by telling James not to dictate where people sit, you've deprived him of sixty percent of his subject matter?"

"Be that as it may," Harris said. "He hasn't told anyone where to sit all day."

———

"Boppo! Look at this!" Jessie shows me her new *Book of World Records*. "It has the Yankees in it!" I say, "So? How many World Series have the Yankees won?" She doesn't need to check the book. "Twenty-six," she says. "Just for that," I tell her, "grab your bags. We're off to Paris for the weekend!" She raises her clenched fists at her sides as though she were carrying suitcases, and trots toward the front door.

———

"You know, Jessie, when I was a little girl . . ."

"Oh, Boppo!"

———◆———

My teaching load for the fall term consists of two courses, and remains light. On Mondays I teach a graduate course in modern poetry at the Stony Brook main campus on the north shore of Long Island, and an MFA course in novel-writing at the Southampton campus on Tuesdays. The Southampton campus is a fifteen-minute drive from our house. Kevin comes over on Tuesday mornings before I go off to teach, and we sit in the kitchen and talk. He never wants coffee or anything to eat. We sit across the table from each other and talk about the Yankees, the Mets, and the Jets (the one team we agree on), or whatever happens to be going on. We also phone each other from time to time.

I come from a society of talkers. He does not. "Do you believe in mediums?" he asks one morning. I tell him no, though not dismissively, because it is clear that he and Cathy want to believe in them. Cathy sees a medium, who connects her with Stephen. Cathy feels that Stephen's spirit is nearby, watching over the family. She reports that lights go off and on in the house on their own to signal Stephen's presence. "I went over to Stony Brook and looked around where he used to walk, and I knew he was with me," Kevin says. I just listen. "I keep paying for his cell phone," he says, "to hear his voice."

Shirley Kenny, the Stony Brook president, has been kind and attentive to the Stakeys, as she has to our family. I only learned of the death of the Kennys' son after Amy died. So many of the people we have heard from during the year have lost children, old and young—many who were friends or acquaintances for years but who had never mentioned the deaths, as if they belonged to a secret club.

Kevin comes over when I am not around, as well. Since finishing the playhouse, he has made other improvements, redoing a section of the third floor so that we'd have a comfortable place for Ligaya in the summers, and shoring up a crumpling part of the basement ceiling, which required rebuilding most of the deck that covers it. I told him I didn't like repair jobs like that because no one could tell how much money was involved. He said he'd put up a plaque on the deck, indicating the cost. Often he comes over just to check that everything is okay.

Today he worries about his fellow builders and contractors on Long Island. "Nobody's building, nobody's using carpenters. The lumber mill in Riverhead laid off over half of its workers," he says. He doesn't know how his friends will survive in the recession. "Do you think Obama will help?" he asks. I say I do. We remain quiet for a while. He says, "Did I tell you I saw a video of Stephen playing his drum in the band?"

———◆———

Ordinarily, I don't believe in teachers letting students in on too much of their private lives. But I intentionally have told my students about Amy and our family situation. The students hear rumors, so my coming straight out with it clears the air, and helps remove the possibility that they will get overly interested in me and not in the material. I do not wish to play the mysterious professor with the unspoken sorrow. Mainly, I'd like them to realize that we're all in the same boat. Every one of them has experienced one grief or another. I tell them about Amy only once.

I like my students this term, which makes for better classes—freer, more far-reaching discussions, and the possibility of surprises. One day, a thoughtful and quiet young woman in my modern poetry class was making a reference to the Metaphysicals. Out of the blue, she said, "I don't like John Donne." Not like John Donne? "He has nothing original to say," she said. I gave her the form-rescues-content argument, but she remained unpersuaded, and I had to admit she may have had a point.

In early November, the class took up Anne Sexton. I had never thought much of Sexton, judging her to be in a minor league compared to such contemporaries as Sylvia Plath and Adrienne Rich. But the students and I were getting into "The Truth the Dead Know," and I liked the poem better than I'd remembered. "This line, 'In another country people die.' What does it mean?" I asked the class. A young man said, "It means that death happens to other people."

---

"So why are 'orchid' and 'cello' alike?" I ask Jessie and Sammy at breakfast. (The Word for the Morning is "orchid." Yesterday it was "cello.") No response. "Think about the 'h,' " I tell them. Jessie says, "The 'h' is silent in 'orchid' but missing in 'cello.' " Sammy says, "But you can hear the 'h' in 'cello.' " I smile.

———◆———

Whenever I get to New York, John and I have dinner. He speaks of Amy with a special melancholy. Amy and Carl, having been less than three years apart, were close in the way of brothers and sisters. John was close to Amy differently. Because she was nine years older, she fluctuated between being a guardian, a teacher, and a buddy. After Carl went off to college, the two of them joined forces. They listened to the same music. They watched *Beverly Hills 90210* and *Melrose Place* devotedly, barring me from watching with them because I made too many blasphemous remarks. One remark was too many. They played the video game *Sonic the Hedgehog.* Amy would kid with John when he was small: "Why are you offering opinions?" she would say. "You're not even a person." John learned the advantages of straight talk from Amy, and the value of friends. He has retained his friends not only from college and high school, but from grade school as well. Ginny and I have a picture of the two of them when Amy was twelve and John three, licking the same ice cream cone in Central Park.

He is even less likely to speak of his feelings than Harris or I, though if I should mention a sad moment I experienced in thinking about Amy, he will allow that he has had similar moments. He plays things so close to the vest that whenever he says something self-revealing, it carries a profound weight. Over dinner at our regular Japanese restaurant a few weeks after Amy died, he told me "I'm starting not to think about her every day. I feel guilty about that." On the dark, cold morning of Amy's burial, we each approached the casket, still above ground. John stood there a very long time, whispering his thanks to her, telling her how much she had meant to him.

Amy's death may have had the salutary effect of instilling a new daring in John. For the past few years, he has been treading water as a paralegal in a firm where he is cherished by people who make his work a pleasure. But they also realize that he has other ambitions that play to his bent as a humorous critic. He has always wanted to write. In the time since Amy died, he has finished his first screenplay, a sharp satire of his generation.

———◆———

November 25, a dank, cool morning in Quogue. Ginny calls on my cell phone as I pull into the post office parking lot. She tells me that last night James cried in Harris's arms. "Mommy," he said, as if calling her. "When is Mommy coming home?" He has never said such a thing. He was just starting to talk when Amy died. All this time, has he been thinking she was simply away? Ginny says Harris told him Mommy is dead and is not coming home, and in the morning James seemed fine. Immediately after we hang up, a friend calls. He asks where I am. I tell him I have to look around to be sure. He thinks I'm joking.

———◆———

A custom in our family, as it is in many families, is to say, "Love you" at the end of phone conversations. "Love you"—with an up-and-down lilt like two musical notes. Amy and I used to talk twice or three times a week. There was rarely anything momentous in our conversations. Once in a while she would ask my advice about whether she should shorten or lengthen her days of practice, or she would mention an injustice in her office. Sometimes I'd ask her to read something I was writing, as I did with other family members. Mostly, we chatted about the children, or made plans for a pending visit. The week before she died, we spoke a couple of times about our coming to Bethesda for Christmas. "Love you."

Carl and Wendy say, "Love you," as do their boys and Jessie and Sammy. Bubbies says it now. "Love you." "Love you, too." Harris also. Lately I say it with certain friends as well as family. Our conversations rise and fall, and I listen for the point where they are winding down to the end. "Love you." Feeling the need more strongly these days, I tend to get it in first.

———◆———

Conversations from outer space: "Daddy!" says Sammy as Harris returns home after an overlong day at work. "I love penguins! I used to hate them, but now I love them!" Harris asks, "Why's that?" Sammy says, "Because I've learned that penguins have enemies!" "That's why you love them?" asks Harris. "And," says Sammy, "I used to think they lived in one place, but they live on sandy coasts and on rocky coasts!"

Jessie to Ginny, while we are riding in the car. "Mimi! Which would you rather do? Have dinner at the White House, or a picnic with your granddaughter?" Ginny says, "Picnic with my granddaughter." Jessie makes a fist and yanks down her arm. "Yes!"

"Boppo!" says Sammy, as he is about to introduce me to his classmate who has come over for a play-date. "This is Cameron! He's Chinese! He eats bugs!" Cameron smiles and nods. "And bees!" says Sammy. "First he kills 'em, then he eats 'em!"

---

We receive Bubbies's first report from the Geneva School: "James Solomon. Date of birth: 9/20/06. Two Day A.M. class—Ms. Franzetti. Fall 2008." Maria Franzetti also taught Jessie and Sammy. She is beautiful, dark-eyed and slim, with a young girl's voice that rolls "R"s in a Latin accent. She sings quite well. She writes: "James adjusted quickly to class. He enters the classroom happily and with a smile. He quickly says goodbye to his grandma and puts his belongings away before going to the kitchen to find the [toy] dogs, and to make [toy] toast for us. He is very vocal and eager to participate in activities. He absorbs everything around him. He enjoys imitating his teachers." A week or so later, Jessie and Sammy bring home their reports, which are through the roof. Mrs. Salcetti and Ms. Merritt, like Ms. Carone, Mr. Bullis, and Ms. Franzetti before them, seem to feel deep tenderness for Jessie and Sammy, not because of what the children have been going through, but because of who they are. Harris, Ginny, and I read the reports aloud. "Mommy would be so proud," we tell them.

———◆———

On December 6, Ginny and I visit the cemetery by ourselves. We go on a Saturday. December 8 fell on a Saturday last year. Monday will mark the anniversary. The leap year accounts for the two-day difference in the dates. Harris and the children will visit the cemetery tomorrow, as will Carl and Wendy. None of us wishes to honor the exact anniversary. We would prefer to commemorate Amy's birthday, and it is unlikely that Ginny and I will go to the cemetery at this time next year, or in the years to come.

The temperature is in the low thirties, the cemetery deserted, the pines laden with shadows. When we stand together in the familiar place, neither of us weeps. We stare at the earth. I lick two fingers and wipe bird droppings from a corner of the marker. Ginny has brought a small bunch of flowers for the cone. We say nothing, and remain standing for five minutes, perhaps ten. "Tell me when you are ready to leave," I say. Ginny turns away and says, "Now."

----◆----

Yet another thing I'd forgotten about children: they relish imitating your least attractive qualities. Sarcasm is especially appealing, as it requires both skill and nerve. Ginny has just offered Jessie more minipancakes for the fourth time. Her persistence is impressive, but it can also be a pain in the ass. She has offered me tea for the forty-six years of our marriage, always receiving the same answer. Lately, I have taken to repeating what the loveable loser says in response to the same offer in *Nobody's Fool*—"Not now, not ever." Ginny says, "More minipancakes, Jess?" Jessie looks at me with mirthful mischief in her eyes. "Mimi," she says. "How many ways can I tell you no?"

Ginny's view of life may not be as unremittingly sunny as it appears, but it prevails in matters such as tea and minipancakes. At her surprise birthday party last year, Wendy's toast recalled the time when she and Ginny were in Amy's kitchen at Thanksgiving, and Wendy had overheated a blueberry pie, charring the crust. Ginny told her not to worry. "It will taste just like *crème brûlée*," she said.

---

One Saturday night, Harris and I go out to dinner at an Indian restaurant in Bethesda. We have a couple of glasses of red wine, and talk about whatever comes to mind—the family, the Georgetown-Memphis basketball game we went to that afternoon, Amy, a little. There is no logic to the relationship of in-laws. The one you love chooses the one he or she loves, and the rest is up to you and that person. Ginny and I feel close to Wendy and Harris, not as parents, but not as friends either—people joined by the presence or absence of a third. Amy's memory binds Harris and me more tightly than if she were alive.

Not a single moment of contention regarding the children has ever risen between us, except of the playful sort. Yet we are both adept at sparring with each other on other grounds. He reminds me of my every practical ineptitude. I remind him of his ongoing six-year-old misdiagnosis of my broken right thumb. Anyone can see it's broken. And it hurts like hell. No matter how often I complain, he continues to dismiss my case as arthritis. It must be very easy to become a hand surgeon these days.

Last week, he surprised everyone by coming home with a new painting. He strode in and hung it in the TV room over the sectional. The painting is of a sunset on a wintry landscape. The trees are black and bare. A frozen stream between two hills leads toward a barren field. The red sky looks on fire. Another time recently, he brought home a large framed photograph of Muhammad Ali in a boxing crouch, admiring himself in a mirror in a gym, and bearing legends that read, "Champions are made from something deep inside them" and "The will must be stronger than the skill." He hung that one in the hall. He has also turned the kitchen table around. It used to stand parallel to the counter that separates the kitchen from the TV room. Harris made it perpendicular. I think he is looking to make things different, or less static.

Yet he seems to want to balance what is changed with what is preserved. When he and Amy went to that medical benefit dinner, a caricaturist drew the two of them the way caricaturists do, with oversize heads and undersize bodies. They are in bathing suits, and Harris is carrying Amy in his arms, in a classic lifeguard pose. He had the picture framed the other day and hung it on the wall near the second-story landing, along with caricatures of the three children, which were done recently. Going up or down the stairs, you can see the family intact.

In some ways, I wish he and I could talk about emotional matters as effectively as we joke with each other. But his emphasis on the positive, which is useful to him, makes it difficult for him to shift gears, even if he wanted to. And I am no better in this. I think I tend to see the darker symbols more than he does. But I am not inclined to talk about my feelings with anyone but Ginny, and only rarely with her. Something about the momentum of our lives is good for us, keeps us from sinking. Given the choice between confessions of sorrow, however cathartic, and the simplest act of getting on with it, we'll get on with it. I only hope that Harris is not wearing down from the pain of Amy's loss. There are no signs of it, but at family events where Amy once shined, he cannot conceal his longing. His face is taut. I will not be his father. He has a perfectly good father of his own. But I worry about him helplessly, like a father.

⸺◆⸺

After nearly a year, Ginny and I wonder whether we ought to ask Harris if he still wants us to stay. We very much want to, and are fairly sure he'll say yes. But we shy away from asking because we don't want him to take the slightest impression that we want out. This is our life. Without Harris and the children to fill it, we would be sitting in Quogue, manufacturing conversations between dark silences. I know we are creating a diversion for the children as well as a differently constructed life for them. Yet we are doing the same thing for ourselves. When Amy died, Ginny and I never had to confer as to where we wanted to be and should be. We had to ask Harris, but not each other. Now, ought we to ask him again? We decide that he will tell us when he wants us to go. And until then, my original answer to Jessie of "forever" stands. If a new woman should enter Harris's life, as we hope will eventually happen, we know he will choose well. When that occurs, we won't have to ask then either.

————◆————

Mrs. Salcetti invites me to visit Jessie's second-grade class, and talk about writing. I conclude that she did not consult Ms. Carone regarding my prior experience. I know Luxmi, Arthur, and Jaraad from last year's first grade. I tell the kids I have memorized all their names, and make up a new name for each of them, calling boys Phyllis, girls Ralph, and so forth. Their cries of protest eat up ten minutes. I look over at Mrs. Salcetti. "Am I through?" I ask. She smiles, and points to the clock. "Only forty minutes to go," she says.

At her insistence, I tell them the plot of my first novel, *Lapham Rising*, sanitizing it a bit, but staying true to the essentials. Naturally, they are way ahead of me. They analyze the characters I merely describe, noting possible nuances. They explain the theme of my book to me. I become adept at nodding. I have them begin a novel of their own. "Write a first sentence," I tell them. "And remember, you want the reader to be very interested right away." Jessie writes, "Once upon a time, there was the best-behaved class in the world." I ask the children, "From that one sentence, what do you think is going to happen in Jessie's novel?" Practically all of them shout, "They're going to be bad!"

Since, once again, it is clear I cannot teach them anything about writing, I decide to lead them in a rousing chorus of "Boppo the Great." They sing it so boisterously, it nearly bring tears to my eyes. I have them do it again, louder, hoping that Sammy will overhear us.

———◆———

When, on another day at Burning Tree, I visited Sammy's class, I decided to drop in on Jessie's class first, to say hello. Her classmate Arthur saw me in the hall, ran ahead, and announced, "Boppo's here!" Jessie's and Sammy's friends all call me Boppo. So do their teachers. One afternoon I was standing by my car, waiting to pick up Jessie after school and take her to a piano lesson. A teacher, whom I do not know, called out, "Boppo! Are you taking Sammy home, too?" I am become Boppo, even in Bubbies's school, where I was asked by the principal to play Dr. Seuss one morning to honor the doctor's birthday. I sat in a rocker, wearing the floppy red-and-white-striped stovepipe, and read *The Cat in the Hat* to two- and three-year-olds. Wouldn't it be fun to see Amy at these moments, standing off to the side of a classroom, hands on hips, making an amused frown. Her father, Boppo the Loud and Absurd. Boppo being Boppo. After a visit to Burning Tree, I walked out to the asphalt parking lot, which was bright with sunshine and packed with cars. Everything dead quiet. No one there but Boppo the Great.

———◆———

Shopping with Carl, I ask how he's doing. The boys are good, excited by the baby on the way. Wendy is in her sixth month. She's going to have another boy (Jessie took the news bravely). Wendy's platelet count is low, as it was when she was pregnant with Andrew and Ryan, but it is being monitored. "No worries, Dad," he says. They are planning to buy a bigger house. "And how are *you* doing—about A?" I ask. Like Ginny, he puts himself last. He says he tears up from time to time, especially when driving. The Christmas songs get to him. "But once or twice a month," he says, "I play that phone message A left Wendy about Christmas presents for the boys, and that helps a lot. Mom has listened to it. Do you think you'd like to hear it now?" I tell him not yet.

———◆———

Carl relates a story about Andrew, who is about to turn six. Andrew is exacting and very hard on himself. If he errs with a single letter when writing his name, he erases the name and rewrites "Andrew" from the beginning. Or he'll take a new sheet of paper and start from scratch. Carl assures him, "Everybody makes mistakes," but Andrew will not accept that.

One afternoon, he was drawing pictures and growing frustrated when he signed his name and made the letters poorly. "Everybody makes mistakes," Carl said. "Not Eric Carle," said Andrew, referring to the author and illustrator of one of his first books, *Brown Bear, Brown Bear, What Do You See?* "Eric Carle's drawings are perfect."

"By the time the books appear and we see them, the mistakes have all been corrected," Carl said. "Everybody makes mistakes."

Ryan, who had been playing nearby, chimed in, "Not

God. God doesn't make mistakes." Andrew said, "God made a mistake with Aunt Amy."

———◆———

Some time has passed since I first called the NYU School of Medicine. Dean Grieco tells me that to date there is over a quarter of a million dollars in Amy's fund, and that it is expected to yield five percent yearly. Alan and Arlene Alda, old family friends, made a munificent contribution. I know even more money is coming in, because friends have told us that their family Christmas gifts to one another were contributions to the fund. "I wish we had Amy instead," he says.

I ask him if our family might know something about the first scholarship recipients. The initial disbursements will occur at the end of January, 2010. He will inquire at the Office of Admissions and Financial Aid, and let me know. He tells me that a reception for scholarship donors will be held at the school in the spring. Would we like to attend? We would.

———◆———

"Boppo, here's a riddle," says Jess. "A man came over on Friday, stayed two days, and went home on Friday. How is that possible?"

"Friday is a horse," I tell her.

"Right," she says. "Here's another riddle. Three men fell off a boat into the water. Only two of them got their hair wet. How is that possible?"

"Friday is a horse," I tell her.

"Right," she says.

———

James awakens at about 10 p.m. and calls for "Daddy." He is not pleased at the sight of me as I enter his room and pick him up to carry him downstairs. "Daddy!" he says. I tell him Daddy is having dinner with friends, and he will be home very soon. He utters a faint "Daddy," but does not despair. Last winter, if Harris was out at night for any reason, and James awakened and did not see him, he would cry ceaselessly until he exhausted himself. Tonight he merely mutters his displeasure, though he remains anxious. "We hear the garage?" he says, meaning that Harris enters the house from the garage after he parks the car. We look for Harris through the front window for a while, then he rests his head on my shoulder. We listen for sounds from the garage.

———◆———

Being without the children is harder on Ginny than it is on me, because I am more used to the effects of solitude. I may have too much time alone, but Ginny, and Harris, have too little. She and I are together in New York briefly, to go to dinner at the apartment of old friends. It has been many months since we last did anything like that. The morning of the day of the dinner, Ginny sits at the end of a couch, her face turned toward the window. I ask her what she is thinking about, not who. She says she is remembering an afternoon when Amy was in high school and the two of them had finished a shopping splurge at Saks. A horse-drawn carriage was standing in front of the store. "We decided to get in and have it take us home," Ginny says. "It was just so whimsical."

She worries that Jessie, growing up without a mother, will be deprived of such experiences. When Amy turned twenty-one, Ginny elicited letters from thirty of her women friends, advising Amy about the nature of womanhood. She, too, wrote a letter, and she collected them all in an elegant book the size of a large photograph album, with pockets on the pages so that one might extract the letters individually. "Jessie won't do those mother-daughter things," says Ginny. I tell her, "She has you. You took Jess around New York and to the *Nutcracker*, the way you took Amy." Ginny looks away. "It's not the same thing," she says.

She is silent for a minute or two. "You know what Harris said to me when we first hugged the day Amy died? He said, 'It's impossible.' It is. It can't be. It's impossible."

———◆———

In her letter on Amy's twenty-first birthday, Ginny wrote that she had always admired Amy's sense of timing. On April 19, 1969, Amy arrived one hour before Ginny was scheduled to be induced. She noted that Amy also had arrived at Boston Lying-In Hospital in style; Ginny and I were driven there in a Harvard police car. And she had arrived with flair. The students in Dunster House lit up the tower that night—one of the few apolitical celebratory events of the spring of the Harvard riots.

"Daddy and I couldn't believe we'd given birth to a girl," the letter went on. Ginny had three brothers, I one, and the two of us had produced Carl. We thought that's what we could do. "Daddy's first reaction was, 'We don't have girls,'" Ginny wrote. "But did we ever make a girl!" When I first saw Amy, curled up in the little white hospital blanket, I recalled what John Kelleher, a professor of Irish Studies at Harvard, and the father of four girls, had told me about fathers and daughters: "Every girl child peers up from her crib, sees her old man, and thinks, 'Sucker.'"

Ginny's letter detailed all that was loveable and quirky about Amy, so it was a long letter. It was written in a hand surer than Ginny's is these days. Since Amy died, her handwriting has deteriorated—one of the very few outward signs of her suffering. The letter closed: "I wish you work that matters. I wish you the joy of great love in marriage. I wish you the beauty and fulfillment that comes from being a mother."

———————

From the outset, Ginny has told me she feels Amy's spirit around us. From time to time I have repeated that thought to the children, but I have felt Amy's spirit only fleetingly. My anger at God remains unabated, and it may be that I do not wish to concede Him anything as good or as kind as providing the superintending presence of my daughter. I know what comfort it gives people to think of the dead as nearby. It would be nice as well to think that the dead are happier to be close to us. But, I am more likely simply to accept Lewis Thomas's idea of an afterlife based on the principle that nothing in nature disappears, and to go no further. The only spiritual thought that has come to me is a kind of prayer to Amy that we are doing what she would have us do.

At Thanksgiving, which we celebrated at Dee and Howard's home in Bethesda, Howard asked me to say grace. I said, "The best one can say about this family is that Amy might be pleased with us."

Then one afternoon, Ginny and I were waiting to meet John at Union Station. He was coming to spend the Christmas holiday with us. We were sitting in the car, looking for him. His train was a few minutes late. I felt a hand touch my right wrist—not softly, so that it might be mistaken for the flutter of a breeze on my sleeve, but definite, like a comforting pat one person might give another. I looked at Ginny to ascertain that she had not done it, but she was turned away from me, searching the crowd for John. I hoped to feel that touch again, but I did not. And I have not felt it since. It might have been a small spasm, an involuntary movement of my forearm. Something like a twitch.

———◆———

One night, as the children are about to go to sleep, Ginny finds Sammy lying on his back on the floor of Harris's study. His arms are spread wide and his tongue sticks out of the side of his mouth. The day Amy died, Sammy was alone with her while Jessie went to get Harris. He tried to get Amy to breathe. He tried to open her eyes. "This is the way Mommy looked," he says. "I'll never forget it. She was so young, the youngest person ever to die." Ginny says yes, Amy was very young and that she was a wonderful Mommy. Sammy gets up from the floor and goes to bed.

———◆———

Wendy's parents, Rose and Bob, bring the children a book called *Elf on the Shelf,* and the seven-inch-high elf doll that accompanies it. The book explains that the elf will sit around the house, observing the children's behavior, and report directly to Santa Claus. The elf is supposed to move to a different location and vantage point every night, so Harris, Ginny, and I give him a hand. He has a red pointed cap, spindly legs, and the squinched-up face of a sneak. I think him little better than a snitch. But Harris notes that since his arrival, the children's behavior has been impeccable. He would like to extend the elf's stay, but cannot think of a justification.

———◆———

On Christmas Day I help Jessie put up *High School Musical* stickers on the walls and closet doors of her room. The morning goes easier than it did last year. The news that nobody is buying anything in this season evidently has not reached the children of Clearwood Road. Besides the stickers, Jessie got books, a snow globe, a karaoke player, lots of clothes, and her own computer. Sammy, who does not regard clothes as gifts, got a remote control motorcycle and rider, a Mars Mission Lego set, Air Hogs remote control helicopters that terrorize everyone in the house, and, for the Wii, Mario

Baseball and a Star Wars game, in which it is possible to make massive gains, and in a trice, to lose everything. The Wii is dazzlingly inventive, and in its own addictive way, it may also teach that disasters come and go, and there's always another game. Both older children shared a basketball set-up consisting of a hoop, a stand, a backboard, and an automated scoreboard that registers points when someone hits a shot. Basketball has temporarily replaced soccer for Jessie as a Saturday activity, and Sammy plays too. They also shared Shrinky Dinks—decals to color and put in the toaster oven where they shrink and metamorphose into spiders and other animals. I am entrusted with the toaster-oven operation. Besides the Caterpillar dump truck James received, and the gas station, and the workbench, and the garage, he got his own toy toaster—"to make toast like you, Boppo," he said.

Except for the penetrating bray of The Wiggles, to which James has grown attached—"fruit salad, yummy yummy"—the day passes pleasantly. James dashes from project to project, like a driven painter skittering over a large canvas, hammering something in one part of the house, shifting something from one room to another. John plays Sorry with Jessie and tells Ginny it reminds him of Amy playing the same game with him when he was little. In the afternoon we all visit Harris's sister, Beth, in her house on Capitol Hill. Beth, a headhunter in Washington, often takes Jessie and Sammy on excursions to her office. She combines the Christmas gathering with a fundraiser for the children of people in prisons by inviting guests to contribute to the cause. She does this so diffidently, half of us forget to make a donation. Beth has inherited her intelligent ardor for charitable projects from her parents. Howard and Dee spend much of the year helping out in Acadia National Park in Maine. Their Volvo station wagon bears the bumper sticker, "My other car is a bicycle." I told them I am planning to make up a bumper sticker of my own that will read, "My other car is a bigger SUV." They smiled charitably.

In the early evening, John, Harris, Ginny, and I sit down to dinner. Harris looks tired, me too. No one says anything about Amy's absence but the conversation feels choppy. I hear Bubbies in the next room repeatedly playing a Hannah Montana CD on the karaoke. He plays "I Can't Wait to See You Again."

Sammy's enthrallment with the Empire State Building began when Ginny and I took him on his special trip to New York, and he saw the building for the first time as we approached the Holland Tunnel. "What's the *second* tallest building?" he asked. He could make out a portion of the Chrysler Building just behind the Empire State.

"Did you know that a gorilla once climbed to the top of the Empire State Building?" I said. "No way!" he said. Once I had mentioned King Kong, I had to get the DVD of the original 1933 version for him, which was presented as a post-Christmas gift. One afternoon, we watched it— Sammy, Jessie, and I. James and Ligaya came and went. I was a little anxious about certain scenes I remembered, such as King Kong casually grabbing a woman out of her apartment-house bedroom and tossing her to the street. I wasn't sure that the children would find beauty in the beast. But I figured that the size of the ape would pre-dominate, which it did. Jessie could take everything but the bleeding of the dinosaurs. At the sight of the oozing black blood, she hid herself under a throw. Sammy loved it all, especially when King Kong pounded his chest in victory. And the climb of the Empire State Building was as good as advertised. James observed that King Kong was "really big."

In the 1970s, there were at least two revival houses in Washington that showed movies like *King Kong*. On the weekends, Ginny and I used to take Carl and Amy to the Biograph and the Key to watch the Hope and Crosby "Road" pictures, and the Basil Rathbone, Nigel Bruce Sherlock Holmes pictures (the source of their Halloween donnybrook), and Hitchcock's *The Lady Vanishes* and *The 39 Steps*. Amy's favorite was *The Philadelphia Story*. It was not much easier to sell our kids on black-and-white movies than it was to explain them to Sammy and Jessie, but once in, they embraced *King Kong*. "Why does he take the lady away with him?" Sammy asked. I told him he wants to marry her. "What do you think of King Kong?" I asked. "He's mean, but he's kind, too," he said.

———

Jessie's unpanicky and reasonable reaction to *King Kong* suggested that, while retaining her unflagging optimism, she is beginning to accept the existence of terrifying things. A couple of years ago, Amy's friend Betsy Mencher asked if she and her husband Andy could take Jessie with them and their daughter Julia, who is Jessie's age, to a community theater production of *Beauty and the*

*Beast.* As always, Jessie was excited. But Amy predicted that she would have a very hard time with the Beast. Jessie could not deal with anything menacing or evil.

"How well Amy knew her children," Betsy told me. The slightly ominous introductory music to the production had barely started when Jessie became alarmed, and within a few minutes she was crying. "I got her out of that theater as fast as possible," said Betsy. "And we went to McDonald's."

Amy knew Betsy well too. When the two friends had graduated from college, Betsy's latest boyfriend had just broken up with her. She would come over to our New York apartment every day, so that Amy could tell her the boy was worthless, and Betsy could do a lot better, and other customary assurances. Adding comfort food to comforting, Amy would serve Betsy her little brother John's mac n' cheese, which came in the shape of dinosaurs. Years later, on a visit to Amy's home in Bethesda, Betsy came across dinosaur-shaped mac n' cheese in the pantry. She asked why it was there. "To comfort my children when they're in a sad or pathetic state," Amy said.

I can hear her saying that. She often had the voice of a comic with a clipped delivery, even when she was saying things that weren't funny. As with any serious-minded comedian, you could pick up traces of tragedy in the most light-hearted story, and when she said something hilarious, her voice hit just the right notes. The family was at the dinner table in Quogue, kidding Harris about sleeping on the floor during a golfing trip to Hawaii. "Harris Makes Do in Hawaii," said Amy, as if stating a title in a series of children's books. She laughed, Harris laughed, everyone laughed.

---

Odd that I seem to know Amy more completely in death than I did when she was alive. I do not know her any better (I doubt that I could know her any better), but there was so much to her life that I was unaware of until now, when I speak with her friends and colleagues and learn of this sound decision or of that small gesture of thoughtfulness. Jean Mullen, Amy's former chief resident, told me that she and Amy happened to have the same set of dishes, and complained of the too-shallow soup bowls. Jean said, "Amy showed up at my door one day, carrying new deep soup bowls for both of us." One sees many good qualities in one's children as they grow into likeable adults, but their stature may remain obscured, because stature is most often measured at a distance. The distance of death reveals Amy's stature to me. My daughter mattered to the histories of others. Knowing that did not prevent my eyes from welling up with tears for no apparent reason in Ledo's Pizza the other day. But it is something.

———◆———

Carl, Wendy, and the boys come over on a Sunday, and we drive to the Air and Space Museum at Dulles Airport. Harris stays home to catch up on work. The museum is a reduced version of the one at the Smithsonian downtown, but easier for us to reach, and, we hope, less crowded. It is crowded enough, and it has a lot for the kids—biplanes, old airliners, stealth bombers, and rides that simulate space capsules and churn the stomach. Sammy spies a concession stand where everything, from the flimsiest keychain to a large model of a rocket ship, seems to be priced at $26. "Will you get this for me, Boppo?" He indicates the rocket ship. I choose this as my moment to impose limits. He has so much already. Over the summer, in Long Island, when we visited the aquarium in Riverhead, he asked for a stuffed gray-and-white shark, which I bought without hesitation. Here and now, however, I have decided to draw the line.

He takes the rocket and holds it in the air to suggest how wonderful it is. I hold my ground. "You don't need it, Sammy," I say. "Besides, don't we have something like it at home?" He says, "But I want it, Boppo." I tell him, "Not today. Let's look at the old planes." He gives the rocket a swoop with his hand. Carl approaches us. "What's that, Sam?" he says. "It's this great rocket," says Sammy. "Want it?" asks his uncle. And before I can intervene, Carl has shelled out the $26. That evening, I report this moral defeat to Harris. "Frustrating. Isn't it?" he says, looking me straight in the eye.

———◆———

Ligaya falls on the ice. A concussion keeps her home in bed for the first part of the week. When she returns, James runs to her. She holds him as he clings to her head, examines and reexamines her face, and rests on her shoulder. For a full two minutes he does not let go. She has been away only three days. Ginny and I share a glance of apprehension. In April and May, Ligaya is scheduled to return to the Philippines to visit her family.

She plans to be away six weeks. I threaten to have her passport revoked.

———◆———

Andrew's sixth birthday party is held at Laser Nation, in Sterling, Virginia. Jessie and Sammy are excited. James goes, too, but he is too little to shoot other children or be shot. At Laser Nation, the kids are armed with laser guns, which are attached to thick vests that light up when registering hits. The kids hunt each other down in a dark catacomb with pipes and gray and black walls. It looks like the interior of a submarine. The wood is painted to look like steel. Red, orange, blue, and yellow teams, designated by the lights they wear, move about the maze after the children have received instructions in the Briefing Room: No running, no physical contact, no unsportsmanlike conduct. Graeme, one of the participating fathers, who is from Australia, says, "No unsportsmanlike conduct? That discriminates against Australians."

This is how children's birthday parties are done these days, though not all occur in warlike surroundings. Last year, Jessie had her party at Dave and Buster's, a sort of junior casino, where kids play interactive games, and Sammy had his birthday at Little Gym, where the kids jump and tumble on mats. The advantage of such places is that there is no cleanup for parents, and the staff runs the show. I find them weird but harmless, though Laser Nation may be pushing it.

I play with Bubbies, then leave him with Harris as I move to the video game area where Caitlin collars me and pushes me around a while, before I carefully deliver her to her mother's care. The video games include "Extreme Hunting" and "Virtual Cop." Never having tried one, I play "Virtual Cop." I draw the blue plastic automatic from its holder, and knock off every bad guy who pops up on the screen. I take to this. My score is "Excellent." A sign appears: "When all life is lost, the game is over."

Having shot as many people as they could, Jessie, Sammy, the birthday boy, and fifteen other children lay down their arms and eat birthday cake. Bubbies joins the bigger kids, and though his head is barely visible above the top of the long table, he looks and listens and shows no sign that he feels out of place in the company of elders. Jessie meets Ella, the daughter of the Australian, Graeme. Ella is not quite six. "I hear an accent," says

Jessie. "Are you from France?" Ella says, "If I were from France, I would be speaking French."

---

Jessie's to-do list, pinned to the music stand on the keyboard. There are boxes to be checked:

- ☐ GET DRESSED
- ☐ BRUSH TEETH
- ☐ BRUSH HAIR
- ☐ MAKE BED
- ☐ CLEAR DISHES AFTER MEALS

---

While I am away one day, Harris calls to report that James has scribbled all over the sectional with a Magic Marker, and that he has been banished to his room.

"Does he have an attorney?" I ask. Like most doctors, Harris hates lawyers.

"He's already been convicted and sentenced," he says.

"Without due process?" I ask. "I think I'll take it upon myself to represent him in the appeal. This case will be a cinch. You can prepare yourself for a nasty civil suit as well."

"Don't bother. We have witnesses," he says.

"Minors?" I ask. "Are there any fingerprints on the Magic Marker? Has he confessed?"

"In a way," says Harris. "But he does not yet acknowledge the magnitude of his crime."

"Then why," I ask, "was he tried as an adult? Which reminds me: Has he been given his one telephone call?"

"Yes," says Harris. "He's going to call *you*."

———◆———

Long ago, I abandoned all hope that I would ever learn anything new again—too few remaining brain cells. Now, thanks to the reading I do with Sammy before bedtime, I teem with information about trucks, boats, planes, cranes, and drilling equipment. Last night, after Sammy and I had discussed the comparative strengths of stabilizers and forklifts, I lay down for a while with Jessie. Ginny had finished two chapters of *James and the Giant Peach* with her, and Harris was in with James. Jessie was ready to pick up another book—*Harold and the Purple Crayon*—which she read to me.

"Harold creates his own world," said Jessie. "Like writers," I said. Jessie has variously wanted to be a writer, a doctor, a fashion model, and an orchestra conductor. "If you decide to become a writer, Jess, you can create anything you like—friends, princesses, monsters . . ." "New worlds, too," she said. "New planets." I said, "Harold not only creates his own world, he lives in it. That's like writers, too. Another way of saying it is that writers *inhabit* their own worlds." Jessie said, "Inhabit. Let's make that tomorrow's Word for the Morning." I said, "Let's *do* that."

We continued talking about all that a writer can create, like Harold. I said that sometimes, when one creates, one does not find what one is looking for right away, and so must keep creating until it appears. He may even have created it before, but lost it, and now must imagine it again. "Like Harold's window," said Jessie. With his crayon, Harold draws first one window, then two, and then an entire city of windows in an effort to discover the window he lost. "Exactly like Harold's window," I said.

Sammy says he wants to be a scuba diver when he grows up, but he also has a bent for inventing. He would like to make a device that sits on top of a helmet and allows people to see invisible things. "Like ultraviolet rays," he says. "And Mommy." I get him some books about Thomas Edison, in whom he expressed interest when I mentioned some of Edison's inventions. One night we huddle over a book about Edison's early years. Sammy is most impressed by the fact that Edison's hair turned white when he was only twenty-three. Reading to him about the telegraph and the phonograph, I try to make the ancient instruments intelligible to him. I read ahead on a page and learn that Edison's wife died when he was thirty-seven, leaving him with three small children. I hesitate, then read the passage to Sammy. He listens thoughtfully but says nothing.

————◆————

On the morning of New Year's Eve, Jessie is the first of the children to come down to breakfast. "I had the most wonderful dream," she says. "I dreamed that Mommy was alive and that she was having a baby girl." I tell her that after my father died, I used to dream that he was alive, too.

"No," she says. "It wasn't like that. I dreamed they took Mommy out of the ground and found that she was alive. There was just a small tear in her heart, and they could fix it."

"Did you speak with her in the dream?" I ask.

"She was talking very lightly. I couldn't understand what she was saying." There is no sadness in Jessie's voice, more like a report of something wondrous. We speak of other things. She looks at the Word for the Morning, which happens to be "rejuvenate."

———◆———

Catherine Andrews, the children's psychotherapist, has her office in her house, one of the seemingly infinite number of handsome houses on serene, tree-filled streets in Northwest Washington. It is the house in which she grew up, she tells Ginny and me, and to which she returned as an adult to care for her ailing father. Her office is furnished for children, with cupboards for stuffed toys and drawing materials and a little table in the center. On a wall near the door hangs a chart of sketched children's faces in a variety of moods. On the way out, children are asked to pick the mood they are in.

We sit around the little table. Catherine is a small, tidy woman in her fifties, the sort of person you can tell secrets to. She has a lovely, comfortable expression and a calming voice not so soft or without authority as to be lulling. She says we are doing everything just about right, but Ginny and I have come to her specifically to learn if there are things we should be doing in response to episodes such as Sammy lying spread-eagle on the floor. "One thing you might do," she says, "when they are recalling how Amy looked in her final moments, is to show them pictures of their mother when she was active and happy." She speaks of three elements of death difficult for children, or anyone, to come to terms with: its universality, its inevitability, and the fact that the dead are unable to function. She says, "Some children cannot understand why a dead parent does not do something to come back to them." They find it incomprehensible, she says, that death cannot be fixed.

To my surprise, she says she believes in the spiritual presence of the dead. She cites instances of evidence, tactile and otherwise. It is clear, too, that she believes in God and that her God does not intercede in tragedies.

"But he weeps for them," she says. I listen respectfully. Ginny and I tell her of our admiration for Harris. We speak of the delicate balances of our family arrangement, and of our attempt to create a role for ourselves between grandparents and parents. She acknowledges the unusual nature of our circumstance but as yet detects no problems we can't manage.

I mention my concern that Harris appears under a strain these days, and that I feel under a strain as well. The month of December has passed heavily. I tell her I keep saying "Amy" when I mean Jessie or Ginny, and that I often feel removed from friends in social situations. She says that one of the delusions of people in grief is that once a year passes, things will start to look up. She reminds us of what she told Harris at the outset, that grief is a lifelong process for every one of us, not just the children. As for the demarcation of a year, "Things actually get worse. You, Ginny, and Harris are now realizing the hard truth that this is how life will be from now on. One year is no time at all."

Near the end of our hour, she speaks of Jessie. She says boys, like Sammy, tend to demonstrate their feelings and leave them behind—what she had said regarding Sammy's school drawing of Amy lying on the floor.

But girls, she says, are more likely to keep feelings under wraps, and to wait till they feel safe to express them. Jessie had been holding back for a while, she says, but at their last session she made a drawing that Catherine calls "a very good sign." It is a tenet of art therapy, she says, that when children draw themselves standing on firm ground with a sky above them, they are feeling secure. Jessie drew herself standing on a hill, with the sky above her and a rainbow around her.

Sammy asks me why we have years. We talk about what a year on Earth consists of. We consult his "Interactive Planetarium," a talking map of the solar system that answers questions. We learn that years differ from planet to planet. One year on Jupiter equals nearly eleven years and ten months on Earth. One year on Neptune equals nearly 165 earthly years.

January 20. "James!" says Ginny. "Do you know who's President of the United States?" Bubbies says, "O-ba-ma!"

A few days later, I begin the new term at Stony Brook. Back to one course, I teach a workshop called "Writing Everything," in which I have the students write a short story, an essay, a poem, and a play. I try to help them see the usefulness of the demands of each form to the other forms. It has been a month since I was last in Quogue. When I get to the house, Kevin has left a gift for me on the kitchen table—a brass plaque with black antique numbers indicating the amount of his bill for the work he did on the deck. When I phone to congratulate him on his joke, he says he'll send me a bill for the plaque as well.

"I have a DVD of Stephen giving his valedictory speech," he says. "Would you like to see it?"

On his regular Tuesday-morning visit, he brings a portable DVD player. We sit side by side at the kitchen table, our backs to the sun, and watch the 2007 Mattituck High School graduation. The little screen shows the graduating seniors—white gowns on the girls, bright blue on the boys. Stephen steps to the podium. He looks a bit like his mother and his father, but has his own handsomeness and a rich, musical voice. The gold valedictorian's medal hangs on a white ribbon from his neck. At ease speaking in public, he does not refer to himself, but rather addresses his classmates. He uses the metaphor of a Monopoly game to recapitulate their high school years—the "currency" of their education, the intellectual real estate they acquired. He says, "At least most of us avoided jail."

He removes his mortarboard and replaces it with Mickey Mouse ears to reminisce about the seniors' trip to Disney World. He turns his back on the audience and faces his classmates sitting behind him. Everyone laughs and cheers. "Where are you and Cathy sitting?" I ask Kevin. "In the front row," he says. "We recorded everything he did at school, even the most boring band concert." His eyes are red.

---

*Sleep, sleep, our little fur child,*
*Out of the windiness*
*Out of the wild.*
*Sleep warm in your fur*
*All night long,*
*In your little fur family.*
*This is a song.*

—from *Little Fur Family*

———◆———

The dead have occupied much of my time this past year—books and poems about the dead, conversations with other families about their dead. I read death into innocent remarks and innocent texts. At the time it feels accidental, but I know it is not. I should try to get away from the subject. It is not infinitely interesting, as thinking about it ends only in a grim shrug. In any case, there is more to do. And I grow weary of my anger.

Ginny and Harris may feel that their lives have prepared them for our current circumstance. I do not. I doubt that my life has prepared me for any situation, because until Amy died, I had always believed that good things would simply befall me. Except for a few disappointments, probably less than my share, I've led a charmed life. I am learning what most people know at a much younger age—that life is to be endured, and its rewards earned. Since my rewards these days lie in the survival of my family, I am content to try to earn them.

But all this comes slowly to me. I have not been a long-distance runner, and now—at the time when my legs are weak and my wind diminished—I need to confront the long haul, which runs counter to my nature. I must train myself to deal with the world as it is, as Amy did, while not treating the assignment as a chore. One of the few pieces of writing I have done since Amy died was a book review for the *Washington Post Book World*. The novel was David Lodge's *Deaf Sentence*—about a retired linguistics professor, Desmond Bates, who is losing his hearing and who is also deaf to life until, against his will, he visits Auschwitz, where the silence teaches him to hear. He reads a letter from a prisoner in the camp to his wife, discovered in a pile of human ashes. One sentence rises up to Desmond: "If there have been, at various times, trifling misunderstandings in our life, now I see how one was unable to value the passing time." As far as I can tell, this is how to live—to value the passing time.

---

Carl and Wendy have decided on a name—Nathaniel A. The A has no period after it because it's not a middle initial. It's A.

---

We proceed into the new year, like any family, marking on a wall in the playroom how many inches the children have grown. Jessie hardly ever plays the drama queen these days. She no longer confuses disappointment with catastrophe, and she recovers from mishaps readily. She reads very well, and I can make more sophisticated jokes with the Word for the Morning. She disciplines herself. Earlier she had grown uninterested in her piano lessons, but she persevered. A new teacher, Maja, praises and encourages her. At a recent practice session, she was playing not just with her fingers, but with her emotions.

She has even moderated her jealousy. She tells me she understands why I play with Caitlin—"she has no one her own age." And, she and Ginny have grown even closer. Harris tells Ginny how Jessie misses her when she is gone. Events like birthdays and a school play, which seem to shout of Amy's absence, leave their marks. Jessie was darkly silent after the play, in which she was a great success. Yet her buoyant nature prevails. And she looks out for her brothers. She rarely quarrels with Sammy, and she is tender with him when he needs that. One night, when I was reading with her, Sammy came in, teary-eyed from contemplating monsters. Jessie invited him to sleep with her in her bed. When James is upset, she sings him "We are the strong men." He had a stomach virus and threw up all over the kitchen. Jessie immediately went to comfort him.

On my most recent visit to Jessie's class, Mrs. Salcetti asked me to talk about *Children of War,* a book I wrote in the 1980s in which I interviewed children in five war zones around the world. Introducing the subject, I told the second graders that one of the sad and difficult things about children everywhere is that they have no power. Jessie raised her hand. "That's not true, Boppo," she said. "We have the power of thought and kindness."

Sammy is able in so many things, he often collides with his own standards. He, too, reads very well. Ginny and I visited his kindergarten class, where many of the children read on an advanced level. He shows a near-scholarly appreciation of things learned. His exclamation to Harris about penguins derived from a school project that culminated in a Penguin Museum created by the class. Sammy led me around the exhibits like a docent. "That's the Emperor Penguin! You can tell because he's got the orange and yellow and is taller!"

He takes to the responsibilities Pam Merritt has

given him. He and his friend Diana are assigned to wheel the shopping cart containing their classmates' lunch boxes to and from the cafeteria. Very carefully, Sammy lines up the boxes beside the lockers. He has also ceased making farting noises by placing his hand on his underarm and raising and lowering his elbow like the pump of a well. He could make the noise using his hands alone, and his knees, too. For a few weeks, that was his principal avocation. Ms. Merritt blamed Harris and me for teaching Sammy the farting trick, but neither Harris nor I could ever do it. We told Ms. Merritt that Sammy was self-taught, a natural.

James is a little boy now. He continues to show a temper and a will. One night when Harris was away, he wanted to sleep with Jessie. "Jessie needs her sleep, too," I told him as I carried him into his own room. He shouted, "Bad Boppo! Bad!" Most of the babyness is going fast. I miss it. He has rejected his booster seat, even though that requires his taking meals resting on his knees on the chair. He is starting to drink from a "big boy glass," instead of the sippy-cup. He requests (and is granted) his own Word for the Morning. He used to have his breakfast toast cut in small squares. Now he wants "real toast"— two halves. He plays Perfection and Connect Four. He is consumed with projects, such as putting keys in doors and in desk drawers, and removing them again, toting an unplugged-in space heater one-third his size from place to place and turning it on and off, standing beside the karaoke and listening, and taking the remote from one TV and replacing it with another, making it impossible for anyone to watch either set. He is the busiest person I have ever known.

In school he plays independently. One morning, Ginny and I were early picking him up, and observed him from the car where he could not see us. He and his preschool classmates were on the playground. He climbed aboard a large, wide, wooden play ship not far from Amy's bench. He wore a blue knit wool Georgetown cap and his silver winter jacket, which hung open. Ms. Franzetti, also aboard the ship, zipped it up for him. At 11:30, the children arranged themselves single file to return to the school building. Teachers guided them, like hovering giants. James studied his feet as he followed the yellow line. They took a class picture in which he looks like a little Etonian, in a green-and-black striped rugby shirt with a white collar and a faux coat of arms on the chest. He wears a vulnerable yet mature expression, and appears to be five or six, not two.

We have the picture propped up on the kitchen counter. "Who's that?" I will ask him. "Me!"—with happy pride. I do not like that picture.

Harris has signed up for golf lessons. A 12-handicap golfer (had he the time to keep score these days), he has carved out Thursday afternoons to take lessons from a pro. Since, as he knows, I do not regard golf as a sport, I pretend to be bored by his decision. But it greatly pleases Ginny and me to see him doing something for himself. He has also taken up snowboarding. Once in a while, he has a late-night beer with friends. Lately, he has begun a round of birthday parties with his Bethesda high-school buddies, who are all turning forty. At his own fortieth birthday, a surprise organized by Carl, I watched him with Matt Winkler, Scott Craven, and Ramy Ibrahim, businessmen who went to Walt Whitman High with Harris. They were laughing about old girlfriends, making tasteless jokes, and looking sixteen again. Early on, he used to grab dinners on the run, as he bathed the kids and got them ready for bed. Now he, Ginny, and I usually dine at the kitchen table like civilized adults, while Sammy and Jessie take showers.

And Ginny? After a day that consists of making and packing Jessie's and Sammy's school lunches, checking that Jessie's homework is in her backpack, and getting her ready to be picked up for Spanish lessons at 8 a.m., and making sure that Sammy is wearing his warm jacket and not the sweatshirt he prefers, taking Bubbies to Geneva, then doubling back to Burning Tree to help out in Sammy's class; after picking up Bubbies and giving him lunch and driving back to Burning Tree to take Jessie to a play-date with Danielle; after getting food for dinner and coming home to check on Sammy and Bo who has come for a play-date, and picking up Jessie at the end of the afternoon and playing with Bubs as he rides his trike, and preparing dinner for Bubbies, Sammy, and Jessie; after going down to the playroom to read to Bubbies and coming upstairs again to go over homework spelling words with Jessie, and making Sammy's and Jessie's schedules for the following day, and having a phone conversation with the mother of one of Sammy's friends who would like him to come over next week; after preparing dinner for Harris, me, and herself; after playing just-one-more game of Uno with Jessie, and seeing that Jessie and Sammy use the bathroom before going to bed, and reading with Jessie, and laying out her and Sammy's and Bubbies's clothes for the morning . . . she kisses the children good night.

———◆———

Late one morning I am alone in the house. I cannot remember another time when this was so. Harris is at work. Ginny is grocery shopping. Sammy and Jessie are in school. Bubbies is at his gym with Ligaya. I am supposed to be writing. Instead, I wander about the empty places—the playroom, the children's bedrooms, the halls. The only sound is the whir of the refrigerator.

One hardly notices the objects in a house when people are present. Now I take interest in Sammy's Redskins wastepaper basket, in Jessie's fish tank, in James's quilt with the trains running across it. The house feels cold. I go to Jessie's keyboard and play a little. Behind me are the kids' chairs from Pottery Barn, with their names on them. I go to the TV room, but do not turn on the set. I go to Harris's bedroom and look at the family pictures on his chest of drawers. I go back down to the kitchen. The refrigerator door is covered with more pictures of the family, and business cards for things the household may need, such as locksmiths and taxi services, and a poison help line, and souvenirs of places where Amy and Harris took family trips. The paper napkins lie slack in their wooden holder. Cheerios cling to the inside of a bowl.

---

*Hi, Wend. It's A. I was just in Toys "R" Us and I, um, got for the boys. . . . I don't know if I should leave it on your machine, if they can hear it [laughs]. Anyway, call me back. I want to tell you something that I got because part of it you saw at my house, and it was, like, "Oh look at that! The boys love these!" And so . . . I told you it came with a whole costume. But anyway, I got them those . . . I don't know. But if you'd already gotten them, I'll just take them back. I just wanted to double check with you. Um. I hope you're following this. [big laugh] I will talk to you later. Bye.*

---

It is March 1, 2009. At 6 a.m., the sky looks smoky. I set the breakfast table and watch TV, while I wait for the children. The weather people speak of the frost-burdened Midwest and of a record snowstorm rolling up from the south. Bubbies patters from his room in his red pajamas with the feet built in. He comes most of the way down the stairs, opens his arms to me, and jumps. We look out the glass door.

"Going to snow," he says.

"Looks like it, Bubs. Would you like a banana this morning?" I ask him.

"Toast," he says. "*Real* toast."

"Real toast it is."

He goes to the table and kneels on his chair. I bring him a sliced banana and toast, along with my own toast and coffee. We eat.

# acknowledgments

*Making Toast* first appeared as an essay in *The New Yorker*, in December 2008. I am grateful to Dorothy Wickenden and Andrea Thompson of the magazine, and especially to its editor, David Remnick, who gave me invaluable advice. My thanks as well to Dan Halpern, as good a friend as an editor, which is saying something.